Marriage Rules!

The Hilarious Handbook for Surviving Marriage

RYAN O'QUINN

Illustrated by Paul Manchester

BroadStreet
PUBLISHING

BroadStreet Publishing Group LLC
Racine, WI 53403
Broadstreetpublishing.com

Marriage Rules!

The Hilarious Handbook for Surviving Marriage

© 2015 Ryan O'Quinn

ISBN 978-1-4245-5092-0 (hardcover)
ISBN 978-1-4245-5093-7 (e-book)

Illustrations by Paul Manchester | www.wilwhimsey.com
Interior design by Chris Garborg | www.garborgdesign.com
Editorial services by Michelle Winger | www.literallyprecise.com

Printed in China.

15 16 17 18 19 20   5 4 3 2 1

Table of Contents

An open love letter to my wife

Dear Heather,

As you well know, I am probably the least likely person on the planet to write a book about marriage. As I type this, we have been married for almost fourteen years, and I'm pretty sure I mess something up every single day. Maybe that is exactly why people need to read this book as a compendium of what *not* to do! Somehow, some way through many years of marriage, and years of dating before that, you still manage to overlook my imperfections and stick with me for better or worse.

When I first met you, I was blown away by your beauty and didn't expect I had a chance, but I mustered up the courage to ask you out anyway. I quickly learned that the beauty you possess on the inside was the most attractive thing about you. And then you became my best friend.

I couldn't imagine a better match for me, and with you I can tackle anything life throws my way. There are so many things you have taught me. I am by far a better man for knowing you. One of the greatest things I have learned is to not take myself too seriously.

Marriage is the family you get to choose, and becoming a parent alongside you has been the greatest joy of my life. In the grand scheme of things, we are just getting started. I look forward to laughing out loud with you every day for the rest of my life. Thanks for all you have given to me: your heart, your wisdom, our silly kids. I dedicate this book to you with hopes that others may learn a little bit along the way and see the comedy in it all!

Ryan

Newlyweds

How you fed each other the wedding cake says a lot about your marriage.

There are a number of ridiculous traditions at a wedding. Some can be explained, and others just don't make any sense at all. What caused people to carry these strange traditions through the years is unknown. Everyone knows about finding something old, something new, something borrowed, and something blue. That one is sweet and fun for the bride. She often gets those things from a relative or bridesmaids. It's a tradition that has been passed down from an old English rhyme in the late nineteenth century and is a sweet symbolic gesture.

There are other traditions that have crept into our culture and, for better or for worse, you will find them at every single wedding reception—the chicken dance, the YMCA song, tossing the bouquet, and the infamous cake feeding.

Sources say the cake feeding tradition between the bride and groom models courtship behavior where animals feed each other tiny morsels of food. That is just weird. Still others say it is held over from when the tradition was tiny wheat cakes baked by the Romans to symbolize fertility and prosperity. Apparently this somehow morphed into throwing the bread cakes at the bride and groom (similar to rice or birdseed today), and that oddly and miraculously morphed into sprinkling the breadcrumbs over the bride's head. Then the bride would shove wheat cakes into the groom's mouth—literally telling him to be more fertile! This is not exactly what I want to think about the next time I see this at a reception, but now you know and you have to think about it too.

Some trustworthy sources say this little ritual of cake feeding is symbolic of how the couple will care for one another for the rest of their lives. This one carries a little more weight with me. Will the husband put a dab on her nose and kiss it off, thereby garnering a collective, "Aww" from a few hundred people? Will she tease him with a bite and then finally let him have a small taste after some prompting from the crowd? OR will it go something like what happened at my wedding?

When it came time for cake cutting at our reception, I carefully contemplated the actions I was about to take and the impact they would have on my beautiful new bride. After all, she had spent hours picking out her dress, getting her hair done, and going through whatever rigorous makeup ritual brides go through on their wedding day. I wasn't about to ruin it by smearing vanilla icing all over God's (and Maybelline's) perfect creation. So I took the perfect amount of delicious cake on my fork to fit her perfect mouth and placed it gently in front of her face so the paparazzi relatives could do their thing. She ate a small bite right on cue.

Then came her turn. I should have known I was in trouble when she picked up the entire piece of cake in her bare hand. She lifted it to my lips, and as some of the cake bounced off my tonsils, her hand continued up my face, plunging cake deep into my nostrils. This brought a roar of laughter and an eruption of applause from the crowd who somehow expected exactly this at our wedding.

I feel like this was symbolic. Not necessarily that I am sweet and she is evil, but more that we love to have fun. We love to make other people laugh, and we rarely take ourselves too seriously. We have been figuratively smearing cake on each other's faces for years and hope to pass on to our kids the same sense of humor and love of life that we share.

Rule #2   You will realize how selfish you really are.

It would be good if there were such a thing as the selfishness police; unfortunately, there is no agency that will give a citation when we are being selfish. I would be incarcerated most of the time if that were the case. Instead, we depend on our spouse to let us know when we are being egotistical, self-absorbed human beings.

Humans are selfish by nature. Don't believe me? Give a kid a toy or a piece of candy. In most cases, their first thought is not to find someone to share it with. Not always, but generally, we are programmed to innately look out for #1. By definition, marriage is the exact opposite. We are to look out for and care for someone else. We make promises before God and our friends to actually put the well-being of someone else before our own. When you get married, it will likely be a whole new way of disruptive thinking that rebuts the very nature of life as you knew it prior to the wedding day.

I know you will find this shocking, but even I (the extremely witty, brilliant, and humble author of a book on marriage) am not as aware in this department as I should be. A few weeks ago, my wife was busy making lunch for the kids. I walked into the kitchen and she handed me a plate of little grilled cheese sandwiches. As I finished the last bite of warm, gooey, cheesy deliciousness, my wife threw her hands up in an "I give up" gesture and said, "That was for the kids!" Oops.

Unfortunately there is no magic that happens at the exact moment the officiant pronounces you husband and wife. It would be great if there were a supernatural spell that occurred and *poof*, you became less selfish and started putting the feelings of your spouse first. But alas, no such luck.

We can count on our spouse to police us, but it would be better if we all started policing ourselves. Try to catch yourself being selfish. Apologize, correct it, and train yourself to think about your spouse's needs before your own on a regular basis. They say (whoever *they* are) that it only takes twenty-one days to form a new habit, so maybe we should all give it a try. After all, there is nothing but a healthy marriage to gain.

Now, if you don't mind, I'm going to go hide that last root beer in the back of the fridge so my wife and kids don't grab it before I do.

Rule #3 Establish control.

There are many struggles couples are faced with throughout marriage. Some are over money, religion, parenting, intimacy, health, and the list goes on. But there is a specific type of power struggle that has affected more marriages than perhaps any other kind of struggle. It is a serious issue that causes strife between husbands and wives, and studies show that it seldom gets resolved. This ongoing conflict is over domination of the remote control.

The power that this tiny device wields is far more complicated than simply flipping channels. If your spouse gets to the remote before you do, your entire evening could consist of rapid channel flipping, stopping on the last five minutes of a movie thereby spoiling the end and rendering it pointless to watch later, failure to fast-forward through commercials, or worst of all, landing on reality programming.

The other night, somehow my wife was able to slip past me, brush her teeth, put on her PJs and snag the remote control before I even knew what was happening. By the time I caught up to her, she had already crash-landed on some reality show about botched plastic surgery and she was transfixed. The next thing I knew, I was frozen in my tracks, unable to turn away until I saw the reveal of the dance teacher's (near unrepairable and previously botched) new nose. I can never get those minutes back and who knows how long it will be until I can close my eyes without seeing the image of skin being sliced and stretched in unnatural ways.

As you bare your TV-watching soul to your mate, you may discover that a Seinfeld addict may not always get along with the Star Trek nerd. Is *Game of Thrones* on your DVR or are you strictly a *Sportscenter* kind of fan? The objective is to find shows that fall into neutral territory. Often you can find common ground in a procedural, sitcom, or late night talk show. This type of compromise, however, is not without its drama.

In our house, it is not uncommon for me to fall asleep part way through one of our "couple" shows, and then my wife is faced with the moral dilemma of finishing the episode without me or pausing the show and waiting for the next opportunity to finish it together as a couple. If you choose to continue on your own, at least have the courtesy to scrub the DVR back to the point where your spouse fell asleep.

I'm not exactly sure what couples fought over prior to the invention of the remote control. Probably which vaudeville act to see, whose public execution to attend, or who was going to draw a wooly mammoth on the cave wall. I hope that one day the two sides can reach an amicable agreement and end the decades-long battle over the coveted clicker.

Rule #4   Don't be surprised by bad habits.

By the time you reach the "walk the aisle" stage, you hopefully know a bit about each other. But you probably don't know the whole story. Spoiler alert: there will be bad habits. Let's just get that out of the way right up front. The perfect angel that is the woman of your dreams will actually go to the bathroom, and it won't be pretty. The hunky guy that swept you off your feet will definitely leave the toilet seat up, won't shave every day, will probably get chubby, will sprout long hairs out of his ears... and do much worse things that I won't mention in a sweet little gift book.

Prepare yourself in advance for every detail of your special spouse to not be 100% perfect. You know this in your mind of course, but trust me, there will be times when you will be flat out surprised. Put that filter in place and don't act too shocked when he or she rattles the windows with a loud burp at the dinner table.

Other things to expect are open-mouth snoring, naval lint extraction, teeth grinding, hogging the covers, clipping toenails while on the potty, and picking teeth in public with a business card. (Hand raised.) My wife called me out on that last one a few weeks ago at the local Japanese restaurant. I thought it was resourceful, but she was not impressed.

Don't be discouraged from openly talking about what annoys the stuffing out of you. Be honest and mature with discussions—unless of course your spouse is just being disgusting; then you have every right to fight fire with fire. The best way to break an undesirable pattern is by holding up a mirror. You'll probably be able to fix a few bad habits as time goes on, but most importantly, it's about accepting each other the way you are.

Rule #5
There will be sickness, health, and some very yucky stuff.

There is a line in traditional marriage vows that says "in sickness and in health." Those five very important words are not to be taken lightly. There isn't time to go into great detail during the ceremony about what that really means, and let's face it, we're a lot more excited to get to the "to have and to hold" part. What isn't explained is sometimes there are going to be downright disgusting things that happen at some point in your marriage.

I am not so good with such things. To say I have a weak stomach is a drastic understatement. If a strong stomach is made out of iron, then mine is made of paper. When it comes to gagging and puking, I have a hairline trigger. It sounds better to say I'm a sympathetic puker, so I am going to go with that. It makes me sound more genteel somehow. Yes, that's it, I'm a sympathetic puker. I first discovered this limitation of mine at a young age.

One day, my best friend Jon and I had school off due to a snow day. My mom came home from her accounting office next door to make us chicken noodle soup for lunch as we rested between playing in the snow sessions. I don't remember the particulars, but I said something at the lunch table that made Jon laugh. As he laughed, he choked. As that happened, he realized that he was most certainly going to regurgitate the delicious chicken noodle soup and it was going to happen immediately. To his credit he made a beeline down the hallway to the bathroom. Of course, like any curious sixth grade boy, I was hot on his trail keeping pace a half-second behind. Jon made it as far as the bathtub and the puking started. As I watched the first noodles shoot out of his nose, an involuntary reaction started from within and I too leaned over the tub, sympathetically joining in on the disgusting upchuck party, unable to help my friend.

As an adult I managed to redeem myself slightly during the first year of marriage. Heather had a really bad bout of the stomach flu and had to be taken to the hospital. I remember wanting to help her and was determined to stay strong. I also wanted to keep our car puke-free when I drove her to the hospital, so I tied a little baggy to her shirt so she could just turn her head to the side and wretch into it. The plan backfired. It turned out there was a hole in the bag. As I later scrubbed the chunky puke out of my floorboard, I thought back to those noodles coming out of Jon's nose, dry heaved once, and was proud of how far I'd come.

Venus vs. Mars

You will compromise on the important things... like old tee shirts.

You will find in many relationships that one spouse is a collector of things while the other is a purger. This can cause a lot of friction in some marriages. I like to think in my marriage we are both fairly reasonable in this department. We can each hold on to a few sentimental belongings without being featured on the next episode of *Hoarders*.

My wife may not 100% agree on the above statement. She moved around a lot growing up and has adopted a "less is more" attitude about things. I totally agree except for extremely cherished items such as my old tee shirt collection. After finding *all* of them piled on a stack of charity donations one day, I presented my case by explaining to her the significance of each and every precious shirt. Several are concert tees, one is covered in paint and memories from building scenery in college, my friend designed one for a fraternity event, and the one with all the holes is just so darn comfortable. It took years to get it in that condition! Some would call it *vintage*. This is where the importance of compromise comes into play.

Once my wife understood how important the shirts were to me she told me to put them back. Okay, so maybe I scooted down some of her clothes to make room for *my* special garments in *our* closet, but I had to keep my drawer clear to fit my NFL hat collection. And I'd put the hats in the hall closet, but that's where we keep the handmade quilts from my sweet mammaw. She made me a special quilt every year since I was a baby and that was—ahem—a while ago.

Perhaps there are a few more things than I originally thought cluttering up the house, but let me tell you it is nothing compared to the barrage of stuff we acquired when the kids came along. I know I'm not anywhere as messy as they are, which makes my stuff fourth in line to get booted. I think my memorabilia is safe at least until the kids go off to college. Then there will be new negotiations and compromises to be made.

Rule #7

A large majority of males suffer from a debilitating sickness (that I just made up) called *finding-impaired*.

I choose to take the scientific approach to my disease. It's a condition that I suffer from and I cannot help, but my wife thinks I can. It's a guy problem and I'm a guy; therefore, I have this condition. I cannot find things. It's not that I don't look. I actually try. I dig around the cabinets and drawers and absolutely try to see things like the baking soda or the salad tongs. They're just not there.

Something happens to the remote control and it is simply gone. Vanished beyond explanation. Then somehow, some way my wife walks over and picks up a book or magazine or reaches between the couch cushions and within seconds, there it is. She does some sort of voodoo magic that I cannot explain.

It's a statistical fact that men are more color blind than women. We are just optically challenged by design. Therefore, I think we should get a pass in this area. It's almost like God wanted us to have a tactical disadvantage to look for things.

The other day I heard my three-year-old son say that he could not find something. My wife told him that he was exactly like his father. See? It's a male thing. Sorry wives, there's no treatment for the symptoms, and we apologize for the difficulty you must endure while helping us cope with this tragic condition.

Rule #8

There will always be a figurative loaded gun pointed at your head.

By now we have already established that women are smarter than men. Inside the human female is a special memory bank that is always ready. Her brain is like cloud storage that always has room. Everything husbands have ever said, done, or thought is automatically stored as ammunition for a later date. All she needs is one little excuse to pull the trigger.

The keyword here is "excuse." If you don't give her a good excuse to use it, those little factoids could lie dormant in her brain for years. But let's face it, there's no way we can navigate our entire marriage without stepping on one or two of those little landmines.

The speed at which my wife brings out of cold storage the fact that I left her waiting for two hours because I didn't want to be rude to an old friend but I didn't mind being rude to her (insert gasp for breath) into the middle of a current argument is mind boggling. Especially because said incident happened over 17 years ago!

I am really surprised that a covert wing of some government spy organization hasn't come knocking on our door to recruit my wife for her supernatural powers of recollection. But perhaps it is because her special ability only works when recalling facts about me. Somehow her ability to remember that most automobiles these days run on petroleum distillate and must be refilled regularly or that her electronic devices must be plugged in and charged nightly has been impaired.

To this day the location of my second set of car keys remains a mystery in her mind, but you'd better believe that if there is a cause for her to bring up the fact that I forgot her birthday the second year we were dating, it will be locked, loaded, and ready to fire.

My advice to you men is to take cover and watch where you step.

Rule #9   Men are genetically designed to be more sick than women.

In our family of five, as soon as the first sneeze, sniffle, or scratchy throat appears, it is the end of life as we know it for at least two weeks. One by one each family member falls, and if by some miracle one of us parents ends up unscathed, you can bet we will try to avoid the rest of the family as much as possible. Or at least that's what I do. I guess my wife is stuck in the trenches no matter how bad it gets.

It's not that I don't care and don't *want* to take care of them; it's just that my wife is so much better at it than I am. I don't know which cough medicine works or the difference between ibuprofen and aspirin. I have no idea what to do for a tummy ache or what to feed a sick person. My wife can simply touch her lips to the forehead of a sick kid and know within one degree how high their temperature is. I barely notice that they're more hot than normal. They always seem hot to me. Kids are like little fireballs running around. Anytime they end up in the bed with us I'm in a puddle of sweat from their radiating heat.

I'd just like to clear up one thing right now. I've heard from a lot of women lately that when their husbands are sick they act like it's much worse for them and men are generally big babies about it. Speaking for myself, it *is* much worse for me. I seriously doubt that my wife understands how truly awful I feel because there is no way she could get up and fix dinner, give the kids a bath, or clean the kitchen if she were as bad off as me. There's no way I can care for another human being, let alone myself, when I am sick. She claims to be ill, yet runs around taking care of everyone and everything like it's just another day.

The only conclusion I can draw is that men are genetically designed to be more sick than women. Not necessarily more often, we just have it worse when it happens. Something about the female's ability to create life probably has a lot to do with it. I'm not claiming to have scientific evidence here, but these are some pretty intuitive observations I have made over the years.

My wife claims that when she is sick I just get annoyed and have said insensitive things like, "Do you have any idea when you're going to be better?" I'm sure I was just trying to get mentally prepared. So maybe I am missing an empathy chip that compels me to bring her some tea or soup when she's under the weather, and I could probably make more of an effort when a family member gets sick, but cut us men a little slack. It's genetics.

Rule #10 Marriage will be easier if you can read minds.

This one I can't reiterate enough, ladies. If there is something you want us guys to do or say, you're just going to have to tell us. I think there's a movie starring the good-looking actor from that doctor show with the impossibly great hair and he has the special ability to read women's minds, or maybe it was the guy from all those action movies... anyway, my point is, that is fiction from a movie and not at all how men work in reality.

Accept this imperfection of ours. We are not trying to torment you and it doesn't represent a lack of consideration for you, either; it is simply near impossible for us to know what is going on in your brain. There is an axiom that says men just read the lines and women read between the lines. I'm not even sure what that means because I don't know how to read between the lines.

We have come a long way from Neanderthals, but let's have some realistic expectations about what we men are capable of. I tried to surprise my wife by taking her out on a date that I planned all by myself. We were going to ride the subway to downtown Los Angeles, find a cool restaurant to eat dinner, and go see a Clippers game. Perfect date in my book. When I finally revealed the plans and it was not the romantic picnic and ballroom dance class she had been imagining in her mind, I was met with some serious disappointment. Apparently she was wearing the wrong shoes for doing a lot of walking and didn't have warm enough clothes. She also really doesn't enjoy surprises. All of this dissatisfaction could have been avoided had she just told me these things, but according to her, it's not special if she has to tell me what to do.

Over time my wife has learned and accepted the fact that I don't know what she's thinking, and if I try to guess it will be much worse. So save time, and for the sake of our sanity just tell us what you are thinking. Leave it in a note, send it in an email, or write it on his arm. Just don't make him play the guessing game. Thank you. And if you don't like this rule, say so. On second thought, never mind. We don't want to know.

Rule #11

Men, give up the grill and go change a diaper.

We have been force fed a ton of gender roles in our lives. Media does it, our parents did it, and we all enter marriage with some sort of preconceived plan for who does what, whether we want to admit it or not.

I was a latchkey kid in the 1970s and '80s and watched a lot of television. As a college student, I did a report on gender bias in marketing. It is amazing to go back and look at some of the commercials and product packaging to see what we were (and are) being subconsciously told to believe. From my research, I found that not long ago, in most marketing avenues, only boys were seen playing with guns and cars. Probably the most telling example of gender bias that I came across was a toy iron and ironing board set that depicted a young girl ironing while a young boy stood behind her looking on with an approving grin.

I'm sure our parents said it before us and their parents before them, but times have changed. Men are cooking (shocker), women are driving racecars, and everything is fair game. My wife did the majority of the remodeling in our home and is the go-to fixit person for everything in our household.

It's okay for dudes to relinquish the grill and volunteer to change a diaper

or do the grocery shopping. And ladies, don't be afraid to pick up the vice grip (I think that's what my wife calls it) and tighten that leaky faucet that's been driving you crazy for months. It not only mixes things up a bit, but also gives both of you a better appreciation for what the other one does.

I'm not advocating that you do it all the time, by the way. She may be a horrible grill master and he may mistake lettuce for cabbage (hand raised), but hopefully you will have a deeper appreciation for each other at the end of the day.

Rule #12
Men are not programmed to function well without a mate.

It's harder for men to be alone than women, which is why my wife says I have to die first. Okay, if you say so, honey. When I have to leave the house for meetings during the day or I'm on the road for a comedy tour, I get really busy and am constantly moving and continually talking to people. My wife is at home with the kids, having absolutely no adult conversations for the most part, but she has learned to adapt. When I come home from work, I occasionally take over the parenting duties to give my wife a break from the house. Within minutes, I am letting the three-year-old video chat with his mom so she can tell him where he left his Transformers toy that morning.

Word of warning, guys: if you don't know where something is in the house, try looking for it first. If you're like me, calling to ask her what I should eat is also not a good plan. I did this once and while my wife was on the phone I went through the entire contents of the refrigerator so she could tell me how to make myself a meal. Even after all that, I still microwaved a tortilla with cheese and ham.

Some dudes will call or text and ask, "When are you coming home?" Again, not a smooth strategy. It will only annoy her and you will not be the hero for staying home. You will just ruin her night and yours by the time she gets back. Google can be your friend in this situation. Suck it up and ask Siri how to make mac and cheese or boil an egg or whatever it is you are trying to do. Your wife will come back eventually.

Rule #13 There are always two versions to every story.

The male and female brains are, of course, equal but apparently laid out a bit differently. One seemingly harmless incident to him may appear to be the end of life as we know it to her. So maybe that's an exaggeration, but you get the point.

My wife and I occasionally encounter these male vs. female discrepancies. One example that comes to mind is an ongoing conflict we have in our household. We love to throw parties and host at our house frequently. I invite friends, set out some napkins, and sweep off the back patio in preparation . As soon as the first guest walks through the door, I proceed to do my duties as a good host. I grab a cold drink, enjoy the delicious snacks laid out, and play some running charades, laser tag, or whatever crazy thing we have set up as the theme du jour. This is precisely why we throw parties: eat, drink, and have fun, right?

My wife has a different point of view. She says her party planning starts way before the day of the party with trying to figure out the guest list, deciding on a menu, and making sure there will be enough food for all the partygoers. Then, on the day of the party, there is frantic last-minute house cleaning, anticipating the needs of all the guests (like food allergies, kid food, etc.), as well as leaving time to do whatever primping girls do before going to parties.

As the first guests arrive, it's a whirlwind of preparing and setting out food, getting the lighting just right, and making sure to pay equal amounts of attention to as many guests as possible. By the end of the night, she's annoyed with me for not helping more, and I think she just needs to relax and enjoy herself.

So I guess what I'm saying here is maybe we can learn something from each other's version of the story. I can help her see that letting go of some of her ideas about what constitutes a perfect party will allow her to have more fun with less stress. She can make me a list (preferably in a smartphone app) of ways I can help before and during the party to take some of the work off her plate. Hey, I may have just solved one of our marital issues by writing this book!

Communication

A long time ago in a marriage far, far away... there were still unspoken battles.

It is a period of marital unrest. The first husband and wife have sent a series of strikes in what will be known as the "Silent Wars." If you are married, you know what I'm talking about. I don't know what the first man and woman fought about, but it has evolved into that unspoken battle when the dishes pile up after a big party, or when there's a suitcase to be unpacked after a long trip. The battle can be fought on many fronts and can be as trivial as who takes the garbage out or how you squeeze your toothpaste.

None of these battles are to be trifled with. A silent war can go on between a couple for extended periods of time and they may resort to guerrilla tactics. It is even possible for one spouse to be in the heat of battle and the other to be completely oblivious to the war raging in their own home.

It was brought to my attention one day when my wife, finally frustrated and defeated, gave up her position amidst a heated conflict (that I was unaware of). Apparently the problem was that I had dressed our recently potty-trained son in his cool baby boxer undies instead of the pull-up he typically wears and placed him in the car to run an errand. Along the way he fell asleep, and it just so happens that he went potty—a lot—in his little boy car seat. My wife was pretty upset, but deciding to be the optimist this time, I didn't think it was a big deal. What I didn't clearly understand or perhaps listen to was the part about what a pain it was to clean the soiled car seat. And thus began the battle.

My wife felt as though I should be the one to take apart the car seat cover and do all the tedious steps required for cleaning. She thought I needed to experience it in order to understand the importance of a pull-up and essentially teach me a lesson. So the battle went on. First the seat was taken out of the car and replaced with the extra backup seat and then eventually moved right square in the middle of the door from the garage to the house. I was probably stepping over it for at least a week. Hints were dropped, to which I was oblivious, until finally holding up her little white flag she told me to go take the cover off the car seat. After heatedly explaining the sordid details of our embattlement she just flat out told me what to do. Hey, that's a thought; just say out loud what you want me to do and avoid the conflict altogether. But that's just me being a guy.

By the way, you wouldn't believe how difficult that ridiculous car seat contraption is to take apart. I was sweating, yelling, and trying to undo all the pieces to that thing, and then I was supposed to know it had to be hand-washed, hang-dried, and put back on the right way. I was ready to throw the whole thing in the trash and buy a new one.

Other than admitting defeat, it is difficult to know who has won a silent war. The conflict is usually quietly resolved and once again freedom is restored to the galaxy.

Rule #15

Your vocabulary can determine your future, so pick up a dictionary.

Good, clear communication is vital to keeping a marriage running smooth and strong. Unfortunately, a lot of problems in this department stem from male vs. female modes of operation. Understanding what the opposite sex thinks can allow you to completely avoid potential arguments.

I am a male. Therefore I am *listening impaired*. That's right. I guess I can hear no problem, but, my desire to listen comes and goes. This one is hard to admit to, because a point goes on my wife's theoretic "I was right" scoreboard. One of the major causes of discord in our relationship is miscommunication of vitally important information. I say she never told me something and she says I wasn't listening, and the cycle continues. We have partially solved this issue with a shared calendar and the use of text messaging (or "trail of proof"), but we're still working on it.

Not all communication issues are listening related. Sometimes it's how we say something, the tone we use, and the consideration for our spouse's feelings that come into play. And sometimes it's something else entirely.

A writer friend of mine with a keen sense of humor shared her story about her would-be fiancé. Early on in their engagement, he explained to her that he had reservations about getting married because he wasn't willing to be monogamous. Shocked, she immediately broke it off but eventually inquired into his rationale behind such a forthright statement. To her surprise she learned that he misunderstood the word "monogamous" to mean "give up your alone time and spend every waking second with your significant other." Not dating other people was not the issue for him at all but apparently the size of his lexicon was a deal breaker for her.

Rule #16

Listen closely. Details are important.

It drives my wife crazy when she tells me something important and I don't listen. Okay, I will go out on a limb and say that most people feel the same way. For example, as I was writing this book, she called to ask if I could bring our daughter's dance clothes to the studio and meet her there because she was stuck in traffic. I agreed, and while she was telling me exactly what she needed, I was engrossed in something else entirely. Apparently the details that she said on the phone spelled out exactly what I was to do:

1. Go downstairs and find the dance bag hanging up next to the garage door.
2. The dance bag is black with rainbow colors and a peace sign emblazoned on the side.
3. Inside the dance bag are jazz shoes and clothes that our daughter needs for jazz class.
4. Bring those items to the studio and in ten minutes.

What I actually heard was something along the lines of, "Get some clothes for dance class and grab her shoes." So I grabbed a shirt that she would wear to school (not dance class), a pair of shorts (not dance attire), and her sneakers (not jazz shoes) out of the closet.

I arrived at the class with items in hand ready to be met with gratitude and adoration for my helpful deed. Instead my wife gave me that look that I have come to know as the "how can you get it this wrong" look. I know and she knows in the grand scheme of things that this is not worth an actual argument. A few exasperated gestures from her and I had learned my lesson. If I had just paid attention, all of this could have been avoided. I'll say it again. Listen closely. Details are important.

Rule #17

Less awesome is less trouble.

Sometimes work takes spouses out of town. Often times these work events will include golf, catered dinners, and extraordinarily plush hotels. When I was on the road, I learned the hard way why I should not lead with this information when calling my wife. I learned to first listen and gauge what her experience at home was before bragging about the killer drive I had on hole seven.

On one such trip I was in Florida doing a comedy and speaking engagement and it had been a magical day, full of jet skiing excursions, eighteen holes of golf, and fresh seafood from the Gulf. I couldn't wait to share my experience with the woman I love and went on for at least ten minutes. I finally summed it up with complaints about how bloated I felt after being served too much food. She then filled me in on her day with my kids. How come when I am away and they are rotten, they are MY kids? Her day consisted of one of our children projectile vomiting, a stage three meltdown by our two-year-old over the color of his straw, forgotten shoes at school drop-off, and an unfortunate incident involving urine landing in my wife's hair. I'm still not clear on how exactly that happened and am not willing to bring it up.

Most of the time, I have a very understanding spouse who encourages me to have fun and take time for myself, but I have learned when I'm away to always let my wife go first when talking about our day, and while I would never encourage a spouse to lie, I might play down the awesomeness of some of my adventures.

Rule #18

Verbal bombs will blow up in your face.

Family life can be pretty tense. There are deadlines at work, kids' busy schedules to keep up with, money stress—all of this can cause tensions to run high. All it takes is one pithy comment and *boom*, a verbal bomb has been dropped, leaving mass devastation in its wake.

I have heard stories from numerous friends about the hairline triggers that set off a catastrophic blast. One in particular that seems to be prevalent is the spouse who comes home from work and throws out, "This place is a disaster." In their mind they've had a long day at work with pushy bosses and boring meetings followed by heavy traffic on the commute home. They're looking forward to walking through the door and being greeted by a warm, loving family and maybe a hot meal. In reality there are dishes piled up, kids fighting, laundry exploded everywhere, and takeout waiting to be ordered. The disappointed spouse mutters these words in a moment of weakness, but what their partner hears is, "You have failed!" being shouted through a gigantic bullhorn.

If we take a moment to imagine the effect these trivial words have on our significant other, we could avoid damage to our marriage that might otherwise be irreversible over time. To help get you started, here are some explosive phrases to avoid:

"This car is a mess."

"The bathroom was clean when I left."

"What exactly do you do around here all day?"

"Is it so hard to put the milk back in the refrigerator?"

"Did you work out today?"

"It takes five minutes to vacuum."

"Will you ever finish something you start?"

"You're not helping; you're actually making everything harder."

"All I do is work and all you do is spend."

"Do you want to go put some makeup on before we go?"

BONUS RULE:

By dropping random positive comments, you can reverse the damage from previous verbal bombs. "Wow, I can't believe how hot you look after such a hard day," or, "Can I take the kids off your hands while you make some of that incredible lasagna I love so much?" For extra bonus points drop something like, "I'm running you a bubble bath after dinner," and wait for the positive ripple effect these utterances will have on your relationship.

Rule #19
Put down the phone and stop pestering her!

My wife and I have an unspoken agreement that when one of us is out with friends, the other spouse does not call, text, or pester the one who is away. We have regular date nights together, but we also understand the need for what we call dude day and girls' night out.

Time with friends is important and healthy for a relationship. My wife actually goes out of her way to make sure I get quality time with the dudes. She's been known to cook up a big dinner for us to enjoy while we sit around the fire pit. In turn, I frequently send my wife out with the girls for dinner or have her escape to a movie in the middle of the day when my schedule permits, so she understands how much I appreciate her. I know how hard she works and what a great job she does mothering our three kids, and it is vital that she feels acknowledged.

Now that I have painted a beautiful picture of wedded bliss, I have to admit I am occasionally guilty of making the phone call five minutes into my wife's first taste of freedom on days where I hold the phone up to my screaming three-year-old and squealing five-year-old so she can hear just how bad I have it in her absence. It's a temptation that is hard to resist. I'm positive the kids never behave like this when they're at home with her. What I actually end up doing is infuriating my wife and negating any positive effect the outing may have had. Put down the phone. Unless there's an emergency, deal with whatever chaos is happening at home and give her the break she deserves.

And ladies, if you love and trust your husband, let him enjoy his time with the guys. Resist the urge to text little doozies like "R u ever coming home?!" or "I hope ur having fun cuz I'm certainly not." If you give him a chance, he may even skip the last tall tale about fishing and take the shortcut home to you.

Rule #20

Wives will walk away, stick their heads in a closet, and try to have a conversation.

My friend Ken Davis says he and his wife have actual arguments using one word: "WHAT?!" In his brilliant comedy routine he says they can't hear each other well, so they just yell "what" back-and-forth until somebody (or both people) gets mad.

I am not saying I am completely innocent, but wives are notorious for walking to the far recesses of the house, sticking their head in the back of a closet, and attempting to ask or answer questions. Ladies, we cannot hear you! You know very well that you accuse us of being hard of hearing anyway. It is much worse when you cloak yourselves in actual cloaks in the back of a wardrobe.

Please understand that we want to hear you and we actually want to communicate. But unless we are right next to you looking at your face and not thinking about sports or sex, it is highly unlikely that we know what in the world you are saying.

Guys, to avoid the fight, get out of the aptly named lazy chair and walk to where she is. Stand next to her and talk to her patiently. Ladies, to keep men from shouting at the top of their lungs and then getting mad about it, simply walk out of the room, stand next to him and have a conversation. Best case scenario: both of you get up from where you are and meet in the middle.

Kids

~~~~~~~~~~~~~~~~~~~~~~~~~~~

Rule #21   **You will learn to embrace the mess.**

My wife and I have young kids. As I walk around the house I look in nearly every corner and all I see is stuff. Art supplies stuff, homework stuff, toy stuff, stuffed animal stuff. Stuff everywhere. How did this happen? I can't really blame it on the kids. My wife and I have a lot of stuff too. We live in a society that simply amasses things and, for better or worse, most of us are just going to have piles and piles of stuff.

Occasionally, I travel overseas and visit child development centers with an amazing ministry called Compassion International. Each trip, I take a suitcase or two filled with our clothes and toys to donate and I realize how little we actually need.

We have a to-do list that never seems to get done and at the top of it is to "get rid of the clutter." The truth is when you have small kids, there's going to be a lot of kid things lying around. My wife and I agreed when we first got married that we wouldn't be those people with all the brightly colored baby contraptions cluttering up the living room. Five years later, when our first child arrived, we bought every crayon colored bouncy seat, swing, and kick mat we could get our hands on in hopes of keeping the baby occupied for even five minutes a day.

Now we have moved on to the Transformers phase. My three-year-old son has discovered these robot toys and they have taken over the house: covering walls with stickers, our minivan with a metal Autobot symbol, and action figures scattered all over the house. They have even caused the cliché dad scenario of me stepping on a sharp robot, falling to the floor, and writhing in pain.

I used to get really cranky and agitated when looking at the chaos. In reality, all of this is just a sign of a lived-in household and is nothing to freak out about. My new attitude is best summed up by a sign some friends have hanging in their kitchen that reads *Pardon the mess. My children are making memories.*

Rule #22 Taking the kids to the store will not earn you points.

If you are not used to being with your kids all day every day, and then you finally take them somewhere by yourself, don't boast about it to anyone in any way. I'm pretty sure I have it worse than my wife when I take all of the kids out of the house by myself. Never mind that she does this every single day of the week. She seems to have no problems taking multiple kids on grocery runs, errands, playdates, etc.

I'm convinced that they are just more difficult when I have them alone. That makes sense, right? They know how to push my buttons. They know just what it takes to upset me. They know when to fight with each other and when to spill things all over the minivan. Surely they don't treat my wife this way.

I have one friend that recently posted a photo to social media when he took all three kids to a big box retailer. He had one kid in a baby carrier on his back, one in the front of his shopping cart and one in the basket of the cart. His caption was something along the lines of *Super Dad*. If it were his wife, the caption would read *Just Another Average Day.* Maybe the right strategy here is to play down the awesomeness of your amazing deeds and you may earn some brownie points at the end of the day.

Trust me when I say it's better for your spouse to just find out that you were a tiny bit helpful, rather than calling a press conference to make the announcement.

Rule #23

Daddy doodie is hard on your own.

I am writing this rule from experience as I have just spent several days straight—alone—with kids. I know, I know, my wife does it every single day and people actually survive such traumatic events. But when you are not used to being in the trenches like this, it can be an eye-opening, exhausting, and rewarding experience. If you are not a stay-at-home parent, in order to get the full experience you must be solo with the kids for at least three days, and one of those days must be a school day.

Even when I took over the parenting duties while my wife was out of town for four days, she put a lot of effort into setting me up to watch the kids on my own. I work full time and I'm not as aware of the kids' daily schedule as my wife, so she made sure the fridge was stocked, and she left sticky notes all over the house to help me keep things running smoothly.

After getting the kids to bed a little late the day she left, I was still secure in the fact that I was fifty percent of this parental setup and I could definitely handle these half-pint humans on my own. The next morning reality hit me as I frantically tried to get three kids out of bed, dressed, teeth brushed, lunches packed, and breakfast made. Then it was shoes on, backpacks packed, and everyone buckled in the car. My neighbor told my wife she counted four separate trips back to the house for forgotten shoes, backpacks, lunchboxes, etc. After two kids were delivered safely to school, I found myself looking at a three-year-old in the back seat not knowing what I was supposed to do with him.

I didn't want to bug my wife and if I may be totally honest, I did not want to reveal that I had actually not paid attention to the instructions she had certainly given me. My wife has a couple of mom friends she does a kid-swap with each week and they take turns watching the preschool age kids while the other moms can volunteer at school or run errands from nine to noon.

Faced with this extra human under my care, I started wondering what day it was and if I was supposed to drop him off with someone or take him home. I really had no idea.

I decided to contact another mom to see if this was the day for drop off. It seemed a little safer than calling my wife. Sure enough, she was ready and waiting and I was supposed to take my son to her house. By the time I had all three kids dropped in the right place there was barely time to go home, do the dishes from breakfast, make a few calls, and then rush back for pickups. I am blessed to mostly work from home and be able to see my kids on a daily basis. I consider myself pretty hands-on, but this was a whole new experience.

By Saturday evening, we'd had our share of ups and downs and I was starting to feel like I was getting things under control. Dinner was cooking and the girls were busy coloring when the newly potty-trained three-year-old had to go potty. After setting him up "dad style" on the toilet with some magazines, I raced back to tend to my pots boiling over on the stove. I was not aware of the degree of supervision my son required when finishing up the process on the potty.

While I was distracted with dinner, he took it upon himself to wipe, smear, and smudge his doo doo all over the bathroom. It was straight out of a horror movie and this required an emergency call to the wife. Aside from talking me down a little, there was nothing she could do to help. I began to tackle the devastation alone. Three rolls of paper towels and a can of disinfectant later, I had a new appreciation for the round-the-clock nature of this full time job my wife has. I highly recommend for spouses of stay-at-home parents especially to try walking a mile in their shoes. You will have a whole new respect for the job.

Rule #24
Tickling your kids is the best thing you can do.

Guys, listen up. I'm sure she chose you for your astonishing good looks, million-dollar smile, and abs of steel. Your confidence and swagger is what got her to look at you twice. But now that you are officially hitched, man cannot survive on a full head of hair alone. I am pretty sure that's Biblical.

At any rate, the best way to keep your special lady friend smiling from ear to ear and getting those butterflies in her stomach every time she thinks about you is... to play with your kids. Trust me on this. Women are wired differently and they absolutely love seeing you on the floor playing with dolls, trucks, or games. I don't care how masculine you pride yourself on being, the moment you pop on a crown and pretend to be a prince while playing make-believe with your daughter, your wife will swoon.

Nobody cares if you dance around the living room that has magically transformed into a ballroom with your little girl and act completely ridiculous.

The same nobodies are not around when you let your son leap off of the couch and on to your back for a wrestling session. It doesn't get any better than that and besides, those kiddos are amazing.

We will all get a little thicker around the middle and lose hair in some places in order to grow it out in others, but you will always melt your wife's heart if you strip away any pretense of being cool and just get down on the ground to play with your kids.

Rule #25

Don't be another one of the kids.

If you don't want to drive your wife crazy, don't act like a bigger baby than your baby. There you go: a nugget of wisdom from a big baby. If you have more than one kid and you've ever gone to a restaurant when they were little, you will know exactly what I'm talking about. If you have multiple kids and get to the end of this entry and are scratching your head thinking to yourself, "I have never had this kind of experience," then put the book down; this is not for you.

Nothing in this world makes the hairs on the back of my neck stand up or sends shivers down my spine as much as when my wife utters these five little words, "Let's go out for dinner." The anxiety comes crushing in around me as I imagine the drinks spilling, the crying fits looming in the air, and the judgmental stares from other restaurant patrons trying to enjoy a quiet meal.

By the time we get to the restaurant, I am so on edge I'm already snapping at the kids before they've even done anything wrong. But I'm just waiting for it, waiting for that moment when everything hits the fan and I can say, "This is why we can't take the kids out to eat!"

My wife is annoyed with me before we have even ordered, and by the end of the meal she drops the "you are worse than the kids" bomb on me that means she is now the only adult in the family. To drive the knife further into my wounded heart she mutters, "I'd rather just take the kids out by myself." Ouch. Okay, so maybe I can get a little worked up and I guess my little anxiety attack could be misconstrued as a tantrum.

I know my wife is with the kids by herself most of the day, and she is used to dealing with misbehaving munchkins in public on a regular basis. I have witnessed her in a hushed tone make an out of control three-year-old stand at attention quivering in their booties. But, in my defense, I don't clock as many hours with our little monsters to acquire this special skillset. I guess I could spend less time freaking out at dinners and learn to embrace the noodles on the floor and the soggy paper straw worms covering the table. Besides, I'd much rather endure the disapproving looks from strangers around me than face the icy stare I'll most certainly get from my wife if I start to meltdown.

Rule #26
You can be a better parent by being a better spouse.

When you have children, everything changes. It's a cliché but 100% accurate. All of a sudden there are other humans to consider in every situation. You have to learn to cope and communicate under incredible amounts of pressure without losing sight of that wonderful person you were when your spouse first agreed to say, "I do."

Unfortunately, sometimes we can go too far with our focus on the kids, and our relationship with our spouse suffers. We only have so much capacity in one day for time, patience, reasoning, attention, and general compassion. Sometimes the feeling is that we only have the energy to take care of either the spouse or the children because at the end of the day we are just too tired for both.

I heard the mother of two small children say that after she puts the little ones to bed the last thing she wants is for one more person to touch her. Men are designed to need physical touch to nourish a healthy relationship, and without it we starve. At the same time, it is important for husbands to realize the strain family life has on moms, and it is vital to give our wives precious time to themselves so they can renew and recharge their energy reserves.

Let's face it, the kids are not going to suddenly become less demanding and recognize that mommy is overworked and daddy needs more attention. They're just not built that way, which is why God made them so cute.

My wife has a friend who is very protective of the time she spends with her husband alone. She makes it a point to always put the kids to bed early so that they have quality time every evening, and the kids end up getting plenty of sleep as a bonus. Even if she goes out for a girls' night, she makes sure to return home early enough to spend time with her husband before bed. That is an admirable attitude to have toward marriage. It is up to us, mom and dad, to make sure our partner is receiving what they need to be happy, and inevitably better, parents.

Rule #27   Sometimes you have to disconnect to reconnect.

Last year my wife and I were invited to a company Christmas party in Colorado. It took a lot of convincing for her to agree to go. She really did not want to leave our kids for more than a few hours, much less a couple days. Finally she relented and then began the task of planning for our absence. Even though we were only going to be gone two nights, I think she started planning weeks out to make sure everything was in order. It required arranging for school drop-offs, pickups, dance rehearsals, and feeding and sleeping schedules. It was no small feat.

Finally the day came and she was a wreck. She was leaving post-it notes on anything that would sit still even as I dragged her out the door. The whole flight there she was dreading the decision to leave them and running through every possible scenario in her head.

Once we landed, got our rental car, and stopped for lunch, things started to change. We actually talked to each other face to face like grownups, used big words, and didn't spell anything. The real turning point came when my wife laid eyes on the hotel. It was beautiful, and we took advantage of all the amenities.

We were only away a few hours in the grand scheme of things but it did wonders for recharging our marriage and was also good for our kids. They got to have a great time with grandma and their aunt and cousins, and I'm pretty certain they stayed up late, ate too much ice cream, and watched cartoons until they fell over.

A temporary disconnect in order to reconnect with your spouse is good for everyone.

Rule #28 Life is what happens when you're busy making other plans.

Marriage is a balancing act and sometimes we put our spouse on hold in order to do other things. Our wives or husbands have been there for us, and we assume they always will be. We sometimes miss our children's important life milestones, even though our intentions are noble.

I heard a story of a man who rarely had time to play with his son and was always traveling for work in order to pay the bills. His son learned to walk and talk while he was away, and the boy longed for his dad to play catch with him or just hang out. The dad missed out on many things all the way through adolescence. Before he knew it, the boy was driving, married, and then had children of his own. The son turned out to be just like his father.

Okay fine, you caught me; it's the story of Harry Chapin's "Cat's in the Cradle." Sorry! We all have jobs and lives and things that demand our attention, but when we put our family on hold in order to take care of other things, it can have unintended consequences. Your life is happening every second of every day—now—so don't have regrets. Take time for those that are the most important. I don't want to miss a thing!

Money

~~~~~~~~~~~~~~~~~~~~~~~~~~~~~~~~~~~~~~

Rule #29

Money matters.

Going into a marriage most people have a pretty good idea of who is the fiscally responsible one. Hopefully you are both financially sound and understand money. That is not always the case, of course, and you need to decide early on in a marriage how to handle your finances.

By the way, this can change throughout the course of a marriage. Early on in ours, my wife was the one who handled all the money and paid the bills. She was the math whiz and this was back when a checkbook was balanced by adding up all the deposits and subtracting all the checks and withdrawals. With paper. And a pencil. We have since switched roles with the invention of computer applications and the birth of our three mind erasers—uh, I mean children—so I now handle the finances. I still rely on my wife regularly to talk through what is going on, make big decisions, etc., but I handle the day-to-day financial aspects of the household.

While we are on the subject, one of my pet peeves is those stupid television commercials around Christmas time where one spouse buys a car for the other. Are you serious?! Who in their right mind, aside from a billionaire, would make a huge financial decision like that and actually purchase a car for a significant other without consulting them first? Correct me if I'm wrong, but both parties need to sign off on all big decisions like that. They make it look super awesome in the commercial and the spouse is always delighted and surprised with the giant red bow on top of a car in the driveway. At my house I'm pretty sure I would be met with a slightly different reaction than a joyful cry and a hug from my wife. It would be more like a furrowed brow, head canted to the side, and a few choice words about why she was not consulted.

A recent survey showed that 47% of the couples polled said their partner has different saving or spending habits than they do. Twenty percent said they have spent more than $500 at least once and never told their spouse. Six percent said they maintain a separate bank account or secret credit card that their husband or wife doesn't know about.

Suffice it to say that money is a huge stress in a relationship and all cards, literally and figuratively, need to be laid on the table early on in the marriage. Even before that trip down the aisle, it would be ideal to know what is owed, from car loans to school debt to credit card payments. Full disclosure now means no surprises later.

Rule #30

Know what type of spender you are.

The way you spend money reveals a lot about your character. It is important to be forthright and honest about this in your marriage. Are you an online shopper—charging purchases to your secret credit card, and having items delivered to your sister-in-law's house so your husband doesn't see? Or maybe you're the kind of consumer who talks about an item, researches it, and then relentlessly obsesses until your wife gets so sick of you she's begging you to buy that hybrid bicycle. Yep, that last one is totally me. Once you have figured out what kind of spender you are, it is crucial to come to some kind of compromise that both of you can live with—or in my wife's case, tolerate.

The majority of my wife's spending is on food. Not eating-out-at-fancy-restaurants kind of spending, but feeding-everyone-in-a-5-mile-radius spending. Early on in our marriage, the sticker shock that came from looking at our grocery bill each month was pretty hard to swallow. Eventually I came to realize that feeding people is a major part of who she is and also one of the reasons I love her so much.

In turn, she has learned over the years how I painstakingly investigate each and every purchase in order to find the absolute best quality and value of a product. Most recently, it was the Golfboard: a maneuverable electric skateboard designed to carry golfers and their gear through eighteen holes of golf while surfing the earth! Okay, maybe that one is going to take a little more convincing (to sell her on its merit) than I initially thought, but I'm not a quitter.

If you really make the effort to come together on this issue you just might learn something from each other that changes you for the better. Our good friend and neighbor shared a story about how she was always the frugal one in her relationship with her husband. While they were dating it really bugged her that he could frivolously spend $40 on a bottle of wine on an average Tuesday night. "I could buy a blouse or pay for a full meal," she'd say. He explained to her that he was paying for that amazing experience to sit with the woman he loved while enjoying a great glass of wine, and it was something he could remember forever. She said it really changed the way she looked at spending money.

Did it solve all of their fiscal conflicts? No, he still zips through the warehouse superstore impulse-buying all the marvelous products they put out on those endcaps while she patrols Pinterest looking for penny-saving, do-it-yourself tricks to save money on just about anything under the sun. But each of them has rubbed off on the other enough to find a little balance, and they're both better for it.

Rule #31

The man will fight for the woman's honor—and finances.

Marriage at its base definition is the joining of two people and two households. We will have "our towels," "our sheets," "our television," and "our money." All of those things sound innocuous except for the last one. Money is very contentious and is a major cause of breakup and divorce. In fact, money and sex are the top two causes. Luckily for you, I cover both in this book. Well, okay, if you are looking for hard data and legit advice, pick up another book, but if you are looking for a good laugh and some marginal advice, keep reading.

I am a big proponent of combining the new family unit's assets into one account. This includes holdings, cars, houses, trust funds, credit cards, secret stashes, and school loans. Sometimes by marrying someone you will come out in the black, and other folks may start out way in the red.

If you love someone enough to commit the rest of your life to them, you have to take the whole package even if it means taking on the awkward debt your wife racked up, pre-marriage, to the guy living across the street. Okay, I suppose I should explain. Don't worry, it's not as bad as it sounds.

A friend told us the story over dinner one night of how when she was dating her future husband, they would take her dog on walks through her neighborhood. Every time they neared a house down the block she would always dart by quickly with her head down. When questioned about this odd behavior, a vague and mysterious answer was always given. Finally after the two were wed, the blushing bride came clean.

It turns out that she had hired the man living down the block to do some gardening for her. Feeling a little put on the spot by her neighbor, she had hastily agreed to let him do the yard work but never settled on a price or payment plan. She admitted that she dreaded getting a bill for his services because she quite frankly couldn't afford it in the first place. The man, however, continued to mow her lawn each week, but never asked for payment. She was secretly hoping after several months that he was still gardening for her out of the kindness of his heart, but alas, a bill finally arrived with a note of hostility. It was way higher than she expected and she simply did not have the full amount to pay him at the time. She was hoping to work out a payment plan of some kind and was surprised to find him still grumpily mowing her lawn each week, all the while adding to the balance of the bill. It had gotten to a point where the man was extorting by way of landscaping, and she was far too intimidated to confront him.

Realizing how stressful and embarrassing this whole debacle had become for his wife, they went together, apologized, and arranged a payoff to satisfy the debt. She now walks by the house down the street with her head held high, but at a fairly fast pace—with no eye contact.

For richer or for poorer means you take on the whole package. Whether it be marrying into wealth or taking on someone's debt, the way you handle this part of your marriage will prove your commitment and support the foundation on which your marriage is built. And for goodness' sake, don't hire a neighbor to do your yard work!

Rule #32

Money makes you blind.

You just got married and as your new life together flashes before your eyes, you suddenly go blind... to money. It is not uncommon to be so caught up in love that you just want to shower each other with lavish gifts like a nice piece of jewelry, or go on romantic vacations, or even go so far as purchasing a home that is out of your budget.

Days after our honeymoon, my wife and I got suckered into one of those timeshare pitches. We were the perfect targets and completely blinded by the idea of our new life together and years of amazing vacations ahead of us. We walked out of the sales room high on life with our ridiculously expensive week of timeshare real estate and a free duffle bag we received as a gift for selling out five of our closest friends and family's contact information. It was an embarrassing and pricey lesson but we learned a lot about making responsible choices. These types of expenditures may serve as a token of love for your spouse, but can also bury you in a mountain of debt if you are not careful.

Next, you start feeling pressure to keep up with those around you. You meet a cool couple in your neighborhood who always seem to be doing something exciting, but their discretionary income for fun outweighs yours by a landslide. I never really related to the old cliché of keeping up with the Joneses until after I was married, but I can now see how easy it is to fall into this trap. My neighbor down the street never fails to roll out the coolest recreational toys every season. In the summer, it's a speed boat and wave runners; in the fall, it's the RV and dirt bikes; and in the winter, he has every snow sport apparatus known to man.

It's especially tricky with kids. We want them to enjoy the same activities as their peers. It seems like the number of extracurricular things kids do now like sports, dancing, music, martial arts, etc. has multiplied by a thousand since I was a kid. My wife and I are learning to set boundaries with the number of activities our kids do to prevent our budget from spiraling out of control.

It's no secret that money issues are a huge strain on a marriage, and it's important to work together on your budget and plans for the future. Keep your eyes open, communicate, and don't feel pressure to equate *love* with *spending*. The best things for your marriage really are free.

Bedroom

~~~~~~~~~~~~~~~

Make time for each other in the bedroom.

I apologize in advance if you were eagerly anticipating this chapter to "heat things up." Perhaps I can recommend a few other titles that will enlighten you on the trendy new ways to make your spouse's toes curl.

No, this chapter is meant to unburden many of us by sharing some of the embarrassing, annoying, silly, and sometimes just plain bizarre things that go on in the marital chamber.

One piece of advice I can give is, after the honeymoon period is over and life "happens," it is imperative that you *make* time to spend with your spouse, alone. You just get preoccupied with other things. It is an excuse we all have. We are busy with work, life, kids, even church, and everything can get in the way of spending time with your mate. Intimate time together is vital to a healthy marriage.

Scheduling intimacy is the tricky part. Maybe you have a code word in the calendar (mine is *amoxicillin*—it's the only word my kids can't spell), or you drop hints throughout the day such as, "Hey, you put on makeup!" or, "Did you finally shower? You smell much better!" There's probably even several apps for it by now.

My favorite method I learned while traveling in Korea: the wooden duck system. Yes, you read that correctly. In South Korea it is customary to receive a set of carved and colorfully painted wooden ducks as a wedding gift. They symbolize commitment because ducks mate for life, but there is another use for them that people have adapted over the years. In the ornate wooden set that you see in homes around Korea there is a male and female duck. Typically the lady duck has a string tied around her beak. Hey, their tradition, not mine. We both know who wears the beak strings in my house... I think.

The best way to illustrate one of the purposes of these ducks is to share a story from missionary friends of mine who were serving in Korea. Shortly after their arrival, they were given a set of ducks as a gift for their new home. Having no knowledge of this particular tradition, they placed the pair on the mantle in their living room facing beak to beak. They invited friends to dinner parties and gatherings at their home and could not figure out why everyone would abruptly leave right after the meal. Finally one bold acquaintance told them that the locals didn't wish to intrude on their "private" time together and would respectfully leave the residence early.

You might have guessed by now that these (genius) ducks signify a spouse's desire for intimacy. I think that is the literal translation. They are commonly set side by side somewhere in the house and the husband points the man duck toward the lady duck to indicate his desire for her affection. If the lady duck is interested she turns her duck facing the man duck indicating it's go time! However, if she turns her tail feathers towards him it is a no-go and he should take a long paddle in a cold pond. I have to say ladies, this is a clear-cut, simplified signal that we males can actually understand. After finally grasping the tradition, my friends moved their ducks to the bedroom and kept their ducky business to themselves.

I'm thinking I should get out my old trusty pocket knife and carry on this brilliant tradition by carving some ducks to help all my married friends. I could give them away as Christmas gifts and kill two birds with one stone! Okay, okay, enough with the puns. My point is this: don't get too busy to get busy.

Rule #34

Males are sometimes required to do a courtship dance.

Men, sometimes your head will be bitten off, but don't take it personally. It happens in nature. I like to look to our fellow animals, insects, and reptiles as a barometer of what acceptable male/female behavior should look like.

For instance, some male spiders perform a special dance when approaching the female, in an effort to avoid being eaten by her. Others will present her with a delicious regurgitated insect in hopes that his head will not be bitten off during or after their "sexy time."

Sometimes those male spiders come home after a long day at work and all they want to do is put their eight tiny little legs up and relax for a minute. Maybe he didn't realize that his sweet spider wife has been home with the hundreds of spider babies all day. His little spider brain should have known better than to come home and start watching the spider nightly news or surf the spider-web (sorry, I couldn't resist). There is spider homework to be done, hundreds of spider backpacks to unload, and spider lunch boxes to empty. Not to mention the spider laundry. Perhaps he should've *started* with the courtship dance. I mean he's kind of asking to have his little spider head bitten off. Why did he have to wait until he saw that she had her eight hands full before he started the dance?

Rule #35
You can't always make them happy, especially in their subconscious.

Sometimes I say or do bonehead thoughtless things and my wife will rightfully call me out on it. Other times I do nothing at all and I'm in the doghouse all day! These types of crimes I have committed against her in her subconscious while she's fast asleep.

Most recently, my wife had stayed up really late making cupcakes for our daughter's end-of-year party. Somehow in her nocturnal psyche, she dreamed that I took one bite out of nine different cupcakes. She woke up angry and went downstairs to see if they were all intact. To her credit, just before bed I did inquire if there were any extras and which ones were for me. In her sleep that translated to me taking a bite out of several of them, therefore not leaving enough cupcakes or time to make more. In reality, she made red velvet cupcakes with homemade frosting and I'm sure they were delicious, but I only got to eat some in her dream.

Even worse than cupcake thieving, I was greeted one morning with the reflection of her icy stare in the mirror as I looked up from brushing my teeth. She was very upset and after a brief confrontation it was determined that I did not actually have another wife and family living in San Diego, and that the plotline to the show she was watching in bed the night before may have influenced her subconscious mind. She eventually apologized, although I still sensed a little hostility from her for the rest of the day.

This rule is simply to serve as a warning. As far as I know, there is no way to combat your spouse's ridiculous subconscious notions, but at the very least I can try to prepare you for the moment when you first get that look of unwarranted disdain.

Rule #36

It's all you dreamed it would be.

Sometimes the craziest things that happen in the bedroom are when you're not even awake. For instance, I found out after I was married to my wife that she is a sleepwalker. I could bore you with weird stories about all the bizarre things she has done, like sleepwalking into the shower at 2 a.m. or occasionally waking up in different rooms, but this one is about something that happened to our good friends Sarah and Dallas.

I'll go ahead and use their real names to sufficiently embarrass them. They have so many great stories on marriage and were my muse for much of this book. Like us, they also have three amazing kids that occasionally drive them absolutely crazy. It's called parenthood. It's normal.

Dallas has about an hour-and-a-half commute to work each way and Sarah is a stay-at-home mom. Like many couples, they don't get a lot of quality time together as husband and wife. They just flat out miss each other because of their busy schedules.

One night after a typical hectic day filled with deadlines, school, commutes, and diapers, Sarah fell into a deep sleep. Dallas later collapsed into bed hoping to get some much-needed shuteye. In the wee hours of the night Dallas was startled awake by his wife's voice whispering, "Don't move." His heart was racing as she repeated in a low whisper, "Do not move." Dallas whispered back, "Is it coming from downstairs?" Sarah again insisted that no one should move. Working up his courage, Dallas slipped out of the bed ready to attack the intruders with whatever makeshift weapon he could find lying around their dark bedroom. As Sarah continued, she mumbled something like, "There's poop everywhere. I need a diaper." The world's biggest eye roll occurred as Dallas plopped back down on the bed, realizing his wife was having a very scary dream about changing a really bad diaper!

That is a definite sign that your wife needs to be swept away for a date night and possibly a day off.

Rule #37

Accept the things you cannot change, like the way your spouse falls asleep.

When listing the ideal qualities you would like in a future spouse, you seldom include their bedtime routine. Bedtime is going to happen every night for the rest of your marriage, and people can develop some irritating habits. While this is not something that should prevent you from marrying your true love, it can cause a great deal of unrest.

My wife and I are the complete opposite when it comes to catching z's. She has trouble falling asleep. Apparently "girl brain" kicks in and she lies in bed staring at the ceiling, making lists in her head and fretting over world issues. I, like most males, am able to put my head on the pillow, pull the covers up, close my eyes, and go to sleep. I don't understand my wife's inability to turn her brain off. My soft fluffy pillow does that for me every time I flop down on it. Once she's actually asleep, however, not even a freight train can wake her up, while the slightest noise jolts me out of bed.

Aside from being a light sleeper, I require vampire-like conditions in order to get some shuteye. There must be complete darkness and silence. My wife, on the other hand, would like to sleep with windows wide open and the sun beaming in on her in the morning to be woken up the way God intended, so she says. Unwilling to use sleep-aid medication, she found that watching TV in bed helps her drift off more easily. Our compromise is wireless TV headphones for her and a plush memory foam eye mask for me.

The important part is to find a reasonable solution you both can agree on. At least these issues can be solved, unlike what to do when you wake up to a drooling, stinky-breathed spouse with a pillow-wrinkled face or pimple cream. *That* I cannot help you with.

Rule #38

There will be accidental peep shows.

The stage is set. There are lit candles, soft music, you are finally alone with the one you love, and the kids are tucked in bed fast asleep... or so you thought. As the two of you embrace for some much needed "mommy-daddy time," your stealthy ninja kid has somehow slipped into the room and suddenly appears bedside at an inopportune moment to let you know he needs a drink of water.

I have heard this story time and time again and the parents are left stammering and coming up with flustered explanations like, "I was helping daddy find a quarter," "We were wrestling," or, "We were building a fort." The important thing to remember here is to take a moment and give an explanation after you regain some composure. If only the home alarm system included a setting for "getting busy" and laser sensors quickly sent an alert the moment those little feet hit the floor. Until then, I suppose an elaborate setup of strings and bells strewn down the hallway could work.

Luckily I have not experienced this mortifying parental rite of passage. I have been warned by others that there is a lock on the bedroom door for good reason. If there is no lock, install one immediately. Good luck to you moms and dads out there, and if it does happen to you, take comfort in the fact that you are not alone. Most likely someone else has been caught in far more embarrassing positions than you. Don't be devastated; it is actually healthy for kids to know that their parents are affectionate. Just try to stick with lots of hugs and kisses with clothes on in front of the children. Otherwise, take it to the bedroom behind locked doors.

Rule #39

Sleep habits should be studied and adjusted accordingly.

It is difficult to know exactly what kind of sleeper you have signed up to share your bedroom with for the rest of your life. The true nature of their habits may not be revealed during the honeymoon phase, but once the covers have literally and figuratively been pulled back, you must now sleep in the bed you have made.

You may have committed the rest of your life to someone who snores like a freight train. The National Sleep Foundation reports that 37 million American adults have a regular problem with snoring. That's a lot of log sawing and that's just one issue. We have a friend whose husband snores so loudly his wife sleeps in a separate room. Perhaps in a case like that, more extreme measures like surgery or gigantic noise canceling headphones should be considered so that no one is losing sleep or gets banished from the marital bed. Most problems in the sleep department can be solved by compromise.

I rarely go to the bathroom in the middle of the night. There you have it. Secret #26 revealed. This is important because, even though my wife and I have never discussed it, she always gets the side of the bed closest to the bathroom. This of course includes our bedroom, but also any vacation hotel, visit to relatives, or anywhere else we happen to be sleeping.

I am also a bedcover hog and I burrow into the bed like a rabbit-eared bandicoot. My wife is perfectly happy with one thin sheet or none at all. My rap sheet also includes teeth grinding and an industrial-sized eye mask to block out the light, while my wife is guilty of sleep walking and talking. All of this would've been helpful information before sharing living quarters. Not that it would've changed my mind about marriage, but now I sort of know what to expect when she starts babbling about Disney characters in the middle of the night or takes a shower for no reason at all. And she has finally adjusted to the fact that I will steal all the covers each night and look like a very comfortable bank robber with my plush eye mask.

Other notable no-no's include the frozen feet fiasco, the pillow swiper, the night sweater, the constant flopper, and the dreaded pet-obsessed bed sharer. Our mattress is usually littered with kids and toys by morning with their tiny arms and legs going every which way. If you don't see eye to eye on all these issues, there will be problems in the marital chamber. A terrible night's sleep means things like circadian rhythms will be thrown off—in lay terms, you will be a crabby human being in the morning and a monster to live with. Do your best to find an amicable way to cope and adjust accordingly.

Better Half

There will be one "friend couple" where you don't like both people.

We've all been there. We've had a buddy or a best girlfriend, and when you found out they were getting married to that person they'd been dating, you faked a smile and said through clenched teeth, "Congratulations." In that moment, it was all I could do to muster up the nerve to lie for the greater good.

There is just no way that every couple friend you have or make throughout your marriage is going to match up with both of you. This is where maturity comes into play. You may have to take one for the team from time to time and put up with the unpleasant person in question. But in an effort to help you through this awkward and nettlesome part of life, I have a few suggestions that might be worth a try.

Avoid double dates. You may have to bite the bullet once in a while, but for the most part make it a guy/girl's night out with the better half.

Fake it. We all deserve acting awards for playing the part of the dutiful spouse. Who knows, maybe over time the wet rag will have a change of heart and become the kind of person you almost enjoy being around.

Get it over quickly. Have the obligatory one or two meals a year and get through it as quickly as possible. You already know it's going to be bad, so just gear up in advance.

Never see them again. You could always come up with great excuses like, "I have to floss the cat." Or maybe something like your wife's aunt Betty is coming over that night, or you are fasting until after the date of their dinner party. This tactic is not ideal unless you totally want to sever the relationship with the cool one as well as the undesirable half.

Invite lots of people. There is safety in numbers, and there's nothing like a bunch of people to act as a buffer between you and that dud spouse to make your get-together more palatable.

I'm pretty sure my wife and I have tried all of the above scenarios. Heck, it's likely that all of these have been tried on us. Either way, you don't always get what you want when you "date" another couple, but that's all part of the compromise we signed up for after we said, "I do."

Rule #41

You will be spun right around.

Any situation can be spun in a positive or negative light. For example, let's say I find out I'm being let go from my job. My first thoughts would probably be that I have failed at my career, I can no longer support my family, we'll lose our house, we'll end up on the street, and I won't have anywhere to store all these books on marriage... that's just where I go.

I've known my wife long enough to know that she would say something funny to lighten the mood, or come up with all the positive possibilities like, "You're getting a chance at a fresh start," and, "You can take your career in a new direction." She might encourage me to revisit a forgotten dream and generally spew her "Pollyanna" attitude all over my pity party. I think she actually makes it a personal challenge to always find a positive outcome from any situation that arises.

We are very fortunate at this point in our lives to live in a nice suburb, but it hasn't always been easy. Early on in our marriage, making ends meet while pursuing our dreams was a challenge, and there were many tiny apartments and sacrifices along the way in order to achieve our goals. Several years into our marriage we decided to save money in hopes of purchasing a home and starting a family. So, we rented a 600-square-foot, one bedroom condo to conserve as much income as possible. It was difficult to downsize, especially considering how much Heather and I like to host get-togethers.

I remember one Easter in particular we had a holiday feast planned for after church with a bunch of our friends and family. I was trying to figure out how we would fit all of them in our tiny home when I got a message from some musician friends of mine who were in town for a weekend performance. Hoping to partake in some Easter festivities, they asked if they could join us. This sent my head spinning, trying to imagine how we could feed and fit the whole band into our humble abode. Unfazed, Heather simply placed out six more plates, cut the food into smaller pieces and opened the front and back doors so that people could spill into the outdoor space. At some point, we all ended up squished together on every square inch of the living room floor playing games. It could have been a stress-inducing turn of events, but with just the right spin, it turned into one of the most enjoyable Easters I can remember.

An important lesson I've learned from my wife is the ever-present ability to positively "spin" my life no matter what the circumstance.

Rule #42

You can't make them something they're not.

If you haven't figured it out by now, my wife is amazing. She puts up with me and she deserves a special place in heaven for all the things I do wrong on a daily basis.

I am slightly obsessive and I go through these little phases where I decide I am going to be into a certain thing or activity. We have gone through various seasons, such as the bicycling years. I decided I wanted us to be a mountain biking couple. I spent lots of time researching the perfect his and hers mountain bikes. I made the purchase and we had several really fun treks through the canyons of Southern California. We even went up the coast and rode in San Francisco, Portland, and Seattle on a road trip. On a biking adventure to Yosemite my wife had an accident and fractured her elbow. No more biking for her, but she gave it her all. Why? Because it was my thing and she loves me.

Later on in our marriage I decided that I was going to get my private airplane pilot license. I bought magazines. I joined the Aircraft Owners and Pilot's Association. Never mind that I didn't actually own an aircraft or have a pilot's license. I watched videos about how to fly and even researched how this new venture would change the premium in my life insurance policy. My sweet and patient wife went along with it and we even went up in a Cessna together as I pursued the dream. Pretty soon kids came along. I decided it was not the best use of time and backed off the notion completely.

Now I know she seems amazingly patient, but in my defense, she knew what she was getting into before we got married. Two weeks before our wedding, I was in the middle of my motorcycle phase and had an accident on the Hollywood Freeway. I was cruising home one evening from work, minding my own business on my awesome new Honda road bike, when all of a sudden everything stopped on the freeway in front of me. I squeezed both sets of brakes and went flying over the handlebars onto the shoulder of the highway. As I jumped to my feet checking to make sure I was still in one piece, what I thought was my right arm swung around, dangling off my chest. It turns out it was just the messenger bag I was wearing across my body and not an appendage hanging by a thread. I then realized I still had two arms and was only scraped and bruised. My motorcycle started again and I slowly made my way one more exit to my house. Without her having to say a word I sold the bike the following week.

Other small obsessions have included surfing, paddle surfing, motocross bikes, pickup trucks, anything Apple makes... you get the idea. Through it all, my wife has been patient. But I have learned that while she has given me the freedom to explore some hobbies, I can't expect her to love it as much as I do. In turn she has introduced me to some things that never captured my interest, such as classic rock, haunted houses, and anything construction-related.

When two people become one it does not necessarily include their hobbies and interests. They will still be separate people. You can't force someone to like what you like. My wife and I discovered together that we both love games. For my birthday last year, we bought a giant laser tag system with ten guns, vests, lights, fog machines—the works. We have continued to add to our collection, and, in the process, our neighbors have gotten involved. They purchased their own arsenal and we have big neighborhood battles.

Our house is the go-to house amongst our friends for games. We play running charades, board games, and video games. We will probably never outgrow these things; that's just who we are. We have an identity both as a couple and as individuals and we know those distinctions.

I'm not sure I will ever completely get a handle on my urge to obsess, but I will try not to force these obsessions on my wife; unless, of course, it's golf. I bought her a set of clubs last month. I'll let you know how it goes.

Rule #43

It's okay to pwn your niche.

If you have no idea what I just wrote above, you are likely not a video gamer. That's okay, neither am I. How do I know the cool-cat lingo? Because my wife is an awesome gamer. She also just told me no one says "cool cat" anymore.

I have heard many marital complaints about one spouse playing video games while the other sits idly by, annoyed and neglected. Typically the husband is the gamer, but in this scenario it's my wife. Video games were never my thing, and although I enjoy playing an NFL or sports-related game from time to time, I have never purchased a console or game equipment for myself. The internal girl programming that would normally make my lovely wife want to go purse and shoe shopping was replaced with a chip that turns her into a killing machine on a virtual battlefield, and I'm okay with this.

Perhaps I can act as a liaison and explain what's going on here (I think they call it the "caster" in game lingo) to all you spouses out there who may feel left out or persona non grata when your spouse settles in for the night with game controller in hand. It's not that they don't care about you or enjoy spending time with you, it's just that they are about to immerse themselves in a world where you no longer exist. Feel better?

My wife started the way many from the '70s and '80s generations did. She grew up on old school systems like Atari and Nintendo NES. She then moved on to a Nintendo 64 and worked her way up to Playstation and XBox consoles. She eventually joined an all-female gaming Halo clan and I don't personally know anyone who can beat her.

I understand the addictive nature of these games and I don't take it personally when she feigns interest in a conversation I'm trying to have with her mid-match. I know she isn't listening to a word I say, but who am I to throw stones? Come football season, I wouldn't know the house was on fire in the middle of a Dolphins game.

The key is to balance solo diversions like game play with activities you can do together. Let your spouse enjoy their time, but if they don't know where to draw the right boundary, let them know how you feel.

Lucky for me, my wife is great at self-moderation, and after our three little ones came along, she cut the controller cord (so to speak) so our kids wouldn't become video game zombies. For now her game-playing days are mostly behind her, but she will occasionally fire up the system to school our friends' teenage kids who come over from time to time. I know hanging up the controller was a sacrifice for her because it was such a big part of her life before our family life became the priority. Maybe when the kids are older she will get back to her former glory of pwning noobs and shattering clichés, and I'll be sitting next to her cheering her on.

Rule #44

Old-fashioned works.

Do not underestimate the power of some old-fashioned traditions. Don't get me wrong, not all traditions should be preserved, like women not being allowed to wear pants or having the right to vote—you know, little things like that. But there are a few historical conventions that should be preserved, and your marriage could really benefit from them.

In days gone by, men were treated like men and women were cared for by their husbands. There were specific roles that each sex adhered to and there was a standard that was expected. The go-to guru for etiquette, Emily Post, suggested that the wife should be sure to greet her husband at the door with a fresh bow in her hair when he came home from work. If my wife did that, I would probably think she was trying to prank me on a hidden camera show. Thankfully we have come a long way in the areas of rights and role changes, but there is still something to be said about the core of those values when husbands take care of their wives and treat them well.

I still believe that the tradition of holding the door for a lady, pulling her chair out at dinner, laying your coat over a mud puddle, and helping her into a carriage is an honorable thing for a real man to do. Okay, maybe some of those things are a little obsolete, but the point is, showing respect to the fairer sex is important to me, and this is what I will teach my son.

On the flip-side, ladies, sometimes you have to remind us Neanderthal men that you demand respect. There is nothing wrong with having high standards when it comes to the way you are treated. My wife is the last person that's going to wait outside for a man to come along and open a door. She is more capable than most males at pretty much every task, but she does expect to be treated like a lady, and I am more than happy to accommodate.

Rule #45 There is such a thing as dinner party etiquette.

As married couples, we often give and get invitations to that age-old tradition known as dinner. It is the adult version of a play date. Apparently this type of grown-up get-together has rules that I didn't know existed until I met my wife.

So just in case you are reading this book and this is new to you, you will now know the official Ryan O'Quinn rules of etiquette at dinner parties. Ok, it's probably easier if I just tell you what *not* to do.

Do *not* come to a dinner party empty handed. Even if the host tells you not to bring anything, (my wife says) you must always bring something. I still think if they expect me to bring something they should tell me. And be specific. Who came up with this polite game of culinary telepathy? Just tell me what you need!

Definitely do *not* bring something that has been partially eaten or left over from your kitchen (unless you are positive it can pass as new). This is apparently considered extremely tacky. I thought it was thrifty and inventive.

Under *no* circumstances at the end of the night are you to pack up and take home the items you brought to the dinner party—unless the host insists you take it home with you and forces the leftover items into your hands as you are leaving. Come on! There's no way they really need to keep my jar of pickles, and are they really going to eat the last three pieces of that bruschetta? No they won't. But I will.

Do not make an uneducated wine choice. I stand there like an idiot in the wine aisle trying to figure out the differences between red and white, and then as a last resort I just phone a friend. Thank goodness for wine snob friends.

Those are really the main rules you need to follow. Bringing an undesirable bottle of Chablis and passing around a re-gifted fruitcake falls into a gray area. Although it is a fairly common practice, it is highly frowned upon and this kind of repeat behavior can land you in the "those people" category. This is another example of how my spouse has taught me to be better. And why she is always in charge of bringing the dinner gift.

Rule #46

You will learn the truth about bad breath.

Leave it to your spouse to tell you the truth. They will let you know when your clothes are wrinkled, your tags are sticking out, your fly is unzipped, there's something gross in your teeth, your hair is crazy, and most definitely when your breath is stinky.

I think all of those things were covered in the "for better or worse" part of the vows, but it's your spouse's job to keep you looking and smelling presentable. If you forget to put on deodorant, your wife will let you know right away. If you forget to brush your teeth, your husband may be the first to report it. Either way, do not take offense.

Thankfully, my wife regularly tells me things that I definitely need to know, and I remind myself that she's just saying it because she loves me—

also probably because she loves other people and does not want me to offend them with horrible halitosis. I love ethnic foods, spicy salsa, raw jalapenos, beef jerky, and anything else pungent that I can eat. All those things are wildly offensive to the human population around me. My wife gives me the brutal facts and tells me to pop a mint. I am thankful for it... and so is the world.

Rule #47
Think before you commit random acts of niceness.

As I have mentioned elsewhere in this book, I need to get better at remembering things. Just to prove my point, I brought my wife some tea when she was sick in bed and it was the only kind that she absolutely loathes. I thought I was doing a good thing! I know she likes tea, especially when she is feeling rotten. I know she wanted tea and probably needed tea, therefore I brought tea. Nope. It's not that simple.

It's not an excuse, but I'm a dude and I'm just not programmed to remember that stuff. It's not that I don't *care* about other people; it's just that I don't *think* about other people. (By the way, don't use that as an excuse with your spouse; it won't come out right.)

As it turns out, the little things are important. Negligible things like your spouse's preferences on tea, food, flowers, movie candy. My wife is so much better at this than I am. It's a good thing she is patient and forgiving.

Given this information, you should do something for your better half *just because*. Daily is preferable, but occasionally is okay, too. Your spouse deserves to feel awesome. Sometimes we need to take an unselfish moment and simply do a good deed with no expectations.

Home

Men want to be on a throne, women want to be on a pedestal, and they both want alone time in the bathroom.

When in the child-rearing years, husbands and wives rarely get alone time. My wife and I have resorted to checking the family calendar to figure out where we are supposed to be next and texting each other important info because there is simply not enough time to sit and talk. It's not an ideal way to communicate, and there are pros and cons to modern technology, but life gets busy and we do the best we can.

Older couples may have the opposite problem. The empty-nesters may spend every waking and sleeping moment together and need a break from their beloved sweetheart. Whatever the case, we humans are certainly designed to be social, but there is also a built-in need for alone time. Sometimes we just need to get away to think. Even if it's a drive alone to the store or an extended potty break, alone time is essential so you can clear your head and be a better spouse.

This includes giving your spouse space and privacy in the primping department. One time after popping in on my wife while she was taking care of a "rogue whisker," (I had no idea this was a thing) she explained to me that stunning beauty doesn't come without a little effort. Before I slowly tiptoed backwards out the door, there was some point made about Esther from the Bible getting twelve months of makeover time before marrying King Xerxes and that she can't even get five minutes to floss her teeth in private. I'm still not sure what she was talking about, but I do know she isn't getting the alone time she would like, thanks to our three kids bursting in on her anytime she's off their radar for more than thirty seconds. I now try harder to give her a respectable amount of privacy.

I once heard the time between buckling your children into their car seats and walking around to the front seat of your minivan described as a "mini vacation." Those eleven seconds are precious and vital.

If you really want to put your man on the throne or your special lady on a pedestal, I suggest making sure they get some valuable alone time. Your life, their life, family life, and your love life will definitely benefit from it.

Rule #49

One of you is merely the puppet.

My expertise in the domestic chores department is definitely cleaning. My wife praises me regularly for my kitchen scouring skills, and like any good puppy who gets a tummy rub from time to time, I keep coming back for more.

I have a system. I start in one corner of the kitchen, work my way around the three countertops, and finally finish with the island. I put things away, I scrub the counters, and I remove the stove eye thingies to wash underneath. I am good.

Not only am I really great at washing dishes, I can pack a dishwasher just perfectly and put the utensils in like a champ. I can even fit ice cream scoops, mixing beaters, and a few dozen forks in that little tray. I'm a pro and my wife is my biggest fan all along the way.

Wait a minute. I'm starting to see the big picture here. Now that I read this, I get the sense that my wife may actually be an ingenious puppet master controlling the entire household for her brilliant schemes.

Could she really be letting me do this because I am so awesome at it, or am I cheap labor? I'm not going to spend too much time thinking about that one. Surely I am just really good and no one can clean the kitchen as well as

I do. Come to think of it, my kids really praise me for straightening their room and putting clothes away. Pardon me while I step away and have a little chat with my housemates. I need to get to the bottom of this.

Rule #50
Sometimes your marriage will stink—like fish.

Everyone has their own ideas about what their little bubble of space should be like in their pursuit of happiness. For me, it's organized and comfortable. I wouldn't call myself OCD, but I do appreciate a clean house, a neat car, the keys to be hung up on those tiny little key hooks in the garage, and my closet to be organized, not just by color of garment, but by shade from light to dark. It's not a lot to ask for and I'm not going to lose sleep over it, but it puts me in a great mood to have my little kingdom in order.

My wife, on the other hand, has a different idea of what is acceptable, or, in her word, *realistic*. I realize that she, as a very active stay-at-home mom who is constantly coming and going with three small kids, has a difficult time counteracting their ability to trash the place at an alarming rate. Sometimes I will clean up an area in our house on a break during the day and somehow my wife and kids will turn it completely upside down just while passing through the room. Do I want to scream and throw my hands up in the air and cry, "What have I done to deserve this?" Yes. But I know that the two dozen cupcakes my wife had to make after dropping off our daughters at school before taking our son to his baby class, and then picking up all three kids to take to their dental appointments is what led to the destruction of our kitchen. Besides, I'd really like to sink my teeth into one of those cupcakes, but if I so much as mention the mess to my busy bride there will be *no* chance of that.

I'm not accusing my wife of being a slob either. Let's just make that clear before I land myself in some hot dirty dish water. She just sometimes makes our kids and having fun with them a priority over cleaning, and who am I to judge?

I do, however, enjoy judging my friends from time to time. Recently our very good friends, we'll call them Sasha and Gene, had an amusing domestic dispute. Gene, like me, also appreciates an unsullied house. He works long hours and when he comes home he wants his castle pristine, especially on days when their house cleaner comes and makes everything look and smell oh-so-fresh. This particular incident incited what my friends considered to be a major fight. Sasha decided to make a lovely fish dinner for her family and thoughtfully grilled it outside on the barbecue, anticipating that the fish smell would stink up the house. Gene excitedly returned home that night expecting to find a freshly cleaned house but instead was smacked upside the head the second he walked through the door by the nasty stench of a fresh catch. Unfortunately, sweet Sasha had opened and prepared the fish in the kitchen and the smell permeated every square inch of Gene's precious sanctuary.

From my lofty perch I could say that Sasha should have been considerate, knowing how her husband felt about the cleanliness of their house and how he worked hard all week and deserved this little piece of happiness. Or I could say that Gene needed to lighten up and recognize that his wife was trying to do it right by cooking the smelly little beast outside—she just wanted to make a healthy meal for her family. But what I really think about this whole scenario is how lucky I am to be friends with the kind of couple where *this* is considered to be a "major" fight. If only all marriages could have such a strong foundation that your major disagreements were over fish. He who walks with the wise, grows wise.

Rule #51   If at first you don't succeed, play more Tetris.

My parents owned a grocery store when I was growing up, and part of the time I was a bag boy. It is not rocket science, but there is an art form to this task. Don't put the milk on top of the eggs, keep frozen foods together, etc. There are tricks of the trade like this that we pros learned with a little experience. In fact, there are grocery-bagging competitions where contestants battle to see who can pack the most groceries in the shortest amount of time. I never competed.

Despite all of my extensive training, I do not pack our car when we travel. My wife is the expert. She is the Tetris queen, and when it comes to spatial relations, my brain just doesn't operate that way. I try it one time and if it doesn't fit I just walk away.

My wife is near genius at this. Recently we were planning to make a television purchase at a big-box retail store. I took one look at the box and started researching the closest U-Haul to help us out. Not Heather. She quickly scanned the dimensions of the box and some sort of super computer in her head took over with all kinds of data and figures racing across her brain. She said, "Yep. It'll fit." Ever the naysayer in these situations (you'd think I would've learned by now), I stood there with my arms crossed, along with

several other store employees as she miraculously tipped the box at an angle, moved seats forward, and with the greatest of precision and not a millimeter to spare, got that thing into the vehicle. We were all amazed and impressed.

She's the best at this. I know it. She knows it. The kids know it, and we all have our roles. About six months ago I gave it a shot again. I tried to pack for a family vacation. I got everything in just perfectly. Just like packing a grocery bag, the heavy stuff was on the bottom, the pillows and stuffed animals were on top. I was so proud of myself. Like a dog waiting for a pat on the head, I waited until just the right moment for my wife to come into the garage and smile proudly at the packing skills I had garnered from her over the years. There was nothing left in the garage for her to pack. I even had room to fit our three kids in the car. I was a man waiting patiently for my praise. She smiled and offered a congratulatory "nice try" as she pointed out that somewhere in the bottom of that precise Lego experiment of luggage were a couple of bags that we needed to have in the front for the trip.

What?! Are you kidding? There was no way to get those bags out. Apparently they contained movies for the kids to watch, drinks for when they were thirsty, and wet wipes for inevitable spills. Ugh. Just when I thought I had done an amazing job, I realized *nope*. I am certainly not the expert here and I should've known better.

Oh well. Don't give up. That won't keep me from apprenticing with the master, and one day soon I may report that I actually packed the car correctly. I'll keep you posted.

Rule #52

Marriage can be a very scary thing.

I was an only child, had a loving mother and father who took care of me, and I grew up feeling safe and secure. My wife's household, however, did not enjoy the same sense of security. She was the youngest of three siblings and readily admits that she terrorized her siblings by hiding for what seemed like hours to scare an unsuspecting brother or sister. She would hysterically laugh and fall to the ground pointing at the horrified face of her victim. I'm sad to report that she has not changed one bit.

Call me crazy, but I expect to walk down the hallway of my home and get from point A to point B without a giant terrifying screechy beast bursting out of the hallway closet and causing me to literally jump straight up in the air and squeal like a little girl. What's worse is now she does it to the kids. The only advice I can give here is don't let them know you're afraid. Once it's out there, the kids will get in on it too. They hide and leap out from the shadows on a nightly basis now. I have nowhere safe left to go. I am lured down the hallway by a child calling for assistance while the other one lies in wait behind the bathroom door, ready to pounce. Now all my wife has to do is walk into a room and I put up my dukes and shriek.

The children have also learned of my fear of detached body parts. Okay that sounds bad. I'm not talking about dismembered limbs necessarily, but other terrible things like loose hairs and toe nails. They use this knowledge to torture me, and others have found out about it too.

One of my best friends and comedy partners, Chris, actually saved up clippings from his and his son's haircuts for months so that he could plant them in my hotel bed when we were on a comedy tour. I will never forget the feeling when I slipped under the covers after a long day of performing only to be covered in thousands of tiny detached human hairs. I just dry heaved a little writing this.

It is simply unfair to have to live this way and I will retaliate somehow, some way, when I stop rocking in the corner, afraid to walk out of my bedroom for fear that one or all of these monsters will make a grown man have to change his pants in the middle of the day (again). If you also are living with this kind of abuse, don't be afraid to reach out to me and share your story.

Rule #53
Dirty Laundry = Stress.

Every week our hallway looks like an apparel minefield. We have a hamper for dirty clothes that can be dried, clothes that cannot be dried, dirty towels, my son's dirty clothes, my girls' dirty clothes and I think a basket of things that have been pottied on. That is at least six different hampers that line the hallway. Inevitably things get pulled out, spilled, and tossed all over the place. I really wanted to include a photograph of our hallway in this book but my wife would not allow it. I think you get the picture anyway, and yours is probably similar.

I have noticed that the laundry (and my wife's inability to accomplish it in one day) makes for big-time stress. She gets frustrated if it doesn't get folded and put away, and everything backs up. Unwashed laundry leads to unwashed dishes which somehow lead to hair clogging the drain, and home life is a nightmare.

My wife graciously took on laundry duties early on in our marriage, mainly because I stink at it. As a kind gesture, I offered recently to wash my own clothes and take at least one basket off her laundry plate. I know it's probably not going to make a huge difference for her, but you have to understand my background in the laundering department.

I am from the South. And I am fairly certain it was actually illegal for men to do laundry where I grew up. It's not something I condone, but it's just the way it was back then. It left me ill-prepared for my future.

Just before my freshman year of college, my sweet mother tried to give me a crash course on laundry, but it was too late. I was too far gone. Dark colors, whites, casuals, delicates. Brain overload. The time finally came when I needed to wash some unmentionables and I realized for that I would need quarters. When I was growing up, my parents owned a store in our neighborhood and I could walk out of my house and go next door to get a candy bar, a carton of milk, read the newspaper, etc. If I ever needed change for a vending machine, life was simple. I just switched out dollars for coins at the family store. So I had a $10 bill and my big college brain knew that I could get a roll of quarters with ten dollars. As I was talking to my mother on the phone I said, "I will send you this ten dollar bill and you send me back a roll of quarters." Mind you, I went to college about 400 miles away from my hometown. When my mother finally regained composure and caught her breath from laughing she reminded me that I could take that same ten dollar bill to a bank or store near me and get a roll of quarters. She also guaranteed that those quarters would work in the laundry machine the same way that quarters from my dad's store would.

So taking all of that into consideration, doing my own laundry is kind of a big deal... for me. At the very least, my wife appreciates the effort on my part, even though I have turned three shirts pink and all my clothes seem to be fitting tighter than I remember.

Happy Wife = Happy Life

Doing something to make her day for no reason at all will give you superpowers.

Like most guys that ever used a towel for a cape, ever since I was a kid I have secretly wished I had some sort of superhuman power like invisibility, healing, or the ability to shoot lasers from my hands. One day I realized that we all are capable of possessing superpowers. Maybe not in the flashy tights-wearing way we see in the movies, but in legitimate qualities found in all my favorite heroes. For instance, I consider my friends who are doctors and nurses to have the superpower of healing. The ability to fly was mastered by some acquaintances who became pilots in the Air Force. Like any good superhero, they bravely soar through the air while protecting us all from harm.

My wife has the superpower to recall the culinary likes and dislikes of anyone she comes in contact with. It's amazing! She knows that my cousin does not like peanut butter but his mom does and egg whites make him gag. One of my best friends has an allergy to beans so they are banished from the house any time he comes to visit. Our kindergartener's best friend can't stand to touch fruit. Not to mention the long, long list of paleo-friendly, nut-free, dairy-free friends and colleagues that regularly gather at our house to break gluten-free bread.

My wife says my superpower is the ability to make people laugh. I have disarmed the angriest of four-year-olds with a simple Goofy impression and rehabbed the hardest of seventh graders with my spot-on imitation of Napoleon Dynamite. The ability to bring a smile to my wife's face is the best of all. With great power comes great responsibility, and I have tried to combine selfless acts with a knack for comedy in an attempt to be a super-husband.

For example, when we were dating I offered to take her dog for a long walk as a helpful, gallant gesture. When I couldn't find a leash (see entry #7 on being finding-impaired), I simply attached the end of my iron cord around the pup's collar and walked her down the street holding the iron in my hand. It actually makes for an excellent leash if you're ever in a pinch. For some reason I was also wearing overalls and I might have been carrying an umbrella...we have pictures. My point is my grand gesture not only sent her into a fit of uncontrollable laughter, but it was a simple, perhaps heroic act to be helpful and make her day.

Rule #55 Coming home early will earn you points and exclamation points!

In many careers, there are certain required times that one spouse will be called away from the home zip code for work. This can be a huge strain on a marriage, but can be minimized if you play the cards right.

My work has a crazy schedule. When people ask what it is that I do, I'm still not sure how to respond. I wear a lot of hats and it just depends on the day. Because of this, I find myself having to travel quite a bit. The schedule, however, is not nearly as bad as it used to be. About two years ago I made a firm decision to pull way back from my travel. My kids were ages five and under at the time and I knew that my first obligation was to my wife and family. Now, given the option, I will always choose to stay home if I can.

When one parent is missing, the dynamic changes altogether in the home. One parent becomes the chef, housekeeper, disciplinarian, and the cuddler. It's just better when there's a second parent around to share responsibilities. There are other entries in this book where I advocate a fair trade off and trust me, I've had my share of single-parenting craziness when my wife has been away for a day or two. By the way, I'm convinced that it is much worse for me when she leaves than vice versa.

With or without kids in the mix, a marriage is designed to have two people. Together. In the same city. In the same house. When one of those is missing it just throws everything off. This is not to say it can't be accomplished effectively; it is just easier to parent with two parents.

Earlier this week I had to be out of town for three days. The timing was very difficult for my wife as she had lots of things happening at the same time. One of our kids came down with the stomach flu in the middle of my absence. When I discovered that we were actually going to end the meetings a few hours early, I quickly started trying to rebook my flight to get home earlier. I even flew into a different airport to make it work and get home a bit sooner. My plan was to make it back in time to tuck in the kids and it actually worked!

I waited to tell my wife of the good news until I was actually seated on the plane and the boarding doors were closed. I have made that mistake before where I thought it was going to work out to get home early and got her hopes up only to find out that it was not possible. This time, when I was finally taxiing down the runway with the plane's nose pointed west, I let her know. I've never seen so many exclamation points in a text!

I'm so glad I was able to make it work. Even if it is just a few hours sooner, your spouse will appreciate the effort, and it especially means the world to your kids when you get to tuck them in.

Rule #56
Men, put her hair appointment in your calendar.

I'm a dude. Generally speaking, dudes pay no attention to anything except for sports and a golf handicap. Admittedly I am the lamest human on the planet when it comes to complimenting my wife's clothes, figure, or hair.

I am making a feeble attempt to resolve at least one third of these by putting her hair appointments into my calendar. Why in the world would I do that? Because I will look at that calendar and remember to compliment her. Otherwise, sadly, I just don't pay attention and will have no idea that she pored through magazines for 45 minutes trying to pick out the perfect 'do to take to the stylist. This way I can at least *pretend* to notice what an awesome new haircut she has.

There are a couple of little harmless cheats that I will also throw in here. By the way, no one has ever written those words in a book about marriage, but I digress. For extra bonus points, look in the family calendar to see if she has included the name of her hair stylist. That way you can say, "Wow, Tara did an amazing job on your hair, honey. You look beautiful." She will be thoroughly impressed.

The second cheat is to snoop around in her purse and see if you can find a folded up photo that she ripped from a magazine to see who it is she is supposed to look like after the stylist works their magic. To accompany the sentence above, you can say something like, "Call me crazy, but I think you look exactly like Cindy Crawford today. Was that on purpose? Because I love it."

Rule #57

You will still need to date your spouse.

Remember when you were attempting to woo your significant other? Whether dudes like to admit it or not, both men and women go through similar rituals of trying to find the perfect outfit for date night. Okay, maybe it's just me, but I doubt it. I would go through a routine of grabbing clothes, trying them on, and throwing the discards on the bed until I found just the right outfit. We probably all spent too much time primping in front of the mirror to make sure that everything was perfect before date night. Ladies, the dudes do it too. I have totally broken bro code here, but oh well.

I am a firm believer that many, many years into marriage, we still need to go out on a date with our spouse. If grandparents or friends don't live close by to babysit, then spring for a babysitter. It's okay and it's important. You need to have one-on-one time with the adult person you committed the rest of your life to. Dinner and a movie is the standard date night in our household. We both love movies and we both love to eat. Voilà!

Take your time, take a shower, pick out great clothes, and don't feel bad about taking a little too long to pamper yourself before going out with your husband or wife. Ladies, that means making sure that you still flirt, and men, make absolutely certain that you open her car door and compliment her regularly.

It will make a world of difference in your marriage if you date your husband or wife even years into marriage.

Rule #58

Clap loudly for your spouse.

Everyone loves to be acknowledged, appreciated, and praised. When our kids do something noteworthy, we encourage them by affirming and praising them. It is also very helpful to them if we do that in front of others. The same rule applies to your spouse. Praise them in front of others. Most of the time, it is your children you are in front of, but not always. Feel free to praise your spousein front of neighbors and friends as well.

This easy practice will do a number of things: first, it will teach your kids how loving parents treat one another and set a great example of marriage for them. It also will show your spouse that you see them and acknowledge their work and efforts at a particular task. Rewards beget rewards. Your relationship will thrive and your spouse will feel better. They will take pride in work, chores, and tasks that may otherwise become mundane.

Go ahead and mention your spouse's accomplishment to others; praise about what they have achieved at work, etc. shows how much you value them. A friend posted on social media that her husband won an award at his job and was named *Employee of the Year*. She boasted that she was proud of him, his hard work, and his accomplishments. I still remember that post and often think of it when I see the couple.

The same can apply to work that typically goes unrecognized. Home chores, errands, kids' carpooling duties. Pointing these out is another great way to acknowledge your spouse and say, "I love you" in a different way. Not that it is bad to say those words at all, but reinforce it in other ways as well.

BONUS RULE:

Take a photo of your spouse when they are not looking and send it to them later. It's not creepy. Ok, it sounds a little creepy, but one guy said he takes random pics of his wife with the kids and sends them to her periodically to tell her how lucky he is. Feel free to steal the idea; I'm sure he won't mind.

Rule #59
Give your spouse a gift outside the box... like Tuesdays.

We had three children within five years. There were several weeks straight where my wife rarely talked to an adult besides me, and I'm pretty sure I don't count. After seeing her stressed to the max and not having a break, I decided to do something about it.

Stay-at-home parents don't get a break. Working parents get some sort of respite in the vehicle going to work, going out to lunch, even sitting in meetings where you don't have people clawing your kneecaps and crying about a soiled diaper. Although sometimes conference rooms *feel* that way, it's just not literally the case. At the very least, when you are at work you can go to the bathroom by yourself. Again, not the case when you're at home with kids.

Now, I realize that our situation is a little different because I also work from home. Not everyone will be able to do this, but you can probably figure out a similar gesture in your marriage.

Two Christmases ago I wrapped up Tuesdays. Yep, you read that correctly. I printed a coupon and wrapped it in a Christmas box and gave my wife the gift of Tuesday. I even put it on the family calendar. Every Tuesday, regardless of what is happening, she gets an afternoon off. Starting at noon she can do whatever she wants. Sometimes she'll call up girlfriends for a nice dinner out or just sit in a quiet movie theater for two hours with a gigantic bucket of popcorn. Whatever she wants to do is up to her. She takes off at noon and doesn't come back home until the sun is down. She says it has helped renew her excitement and attitude toward parenting.

My Bad

Rule #60

Toothpaste can make or break your marriage.

When you combine households for the first time, there are a lot of things you will learn—not only about each other, but about life. My wife has taught me so many things I never knew. Most of them are how *she* does things. I have adopted little tricks and tips and household hacks from my wife that were never on my radar as a bachelor.

For example, there was a problem between my wife and me that has probably plagued many couples for decades: how we squeeze the toothpaste from the tube. Cue the super dramatic *dum dum dum* sound effect. Apparently I have been driving her crazy for years because I squeezed the toothpaste out from the top. She says she never brought it up because it seemed so ridiculous. According to her, when I was finally confronted about this intolerable behavior, every day she would spend a little bit of time tediously squeezing the goop to the top of the container, being sure to press solely from the bottom of the tube, only to find at the next brushing that all the toothpaste was squished back down to the bottom, forcing her to repeat this painstaking process multiple times a day.

Hey, I was just squeezing toothpaste out of a tube. It never occurred to me that there could be this much nuance to something as mundane as tooth brushing. But once confronted, we were able to find a reasonable solution: we just buy two separate tubes of toothpaste.

A few other things I have learned over the years is how to tuck hospital corners when making a bed (my mother-in-law is a nurse), making the bed with the top sheet facing down (this makes no sense to me), and installing the toilet paper roll so that the paper hangs over the top. I would just hang the toilet paper roll whatever way I happened to have it in my hand, but people are very serious about the logic of this one. There are online forums dedicated to such nonsense.

I also learned the hard way that there is a difference between dish soap and dishwasher soap. You *cannot* put dish soap into the dishwasher without it turning into one of those cartoons where bubbles fill the room. Oh, and apparently cabbage and lettuce are not the same thing at all—and only one of them tastes good on a hamburger. This is, by the way, a surefire way to get out of supermarket runs. On the flipside, my wife has learned a few important things from me, such as the advantage to filling up the gas tank *before* the needle is just below empty, the impact moving the extra point to the 15-yard line has had on the NFL, and how to master the art of making fake-gun sound effects. Eh, ok, I guess there's still time for her to learn something.

Rule #61

Resist the urge to spell check your spouse.

My third grade spelling bee still haunts me to this day. It was down to me and Jodi Street in the finals. One of us was going to take home the gold. I was poised to grab that first place prize and dance around the room in triumph when I was given the word "twelfth." What a dumb word. *Twelfth!* I don't like that word to this day. Jodi took home the trophy and I will forever remember that twelfth does *not* have a v.

After that tragic day, mastering orthography has been an objective of mine. Striving to correct my spelling and the spelling of those around me has become my personal mission. But under no circumstances should you ever correct the spelling on the to-do list post-it note your wife left for you and then point those misspellings out to her. I learned that one the hard way and the reaction it evoked... well, I can't even put it into words.

Thanks to spell check, a few additional words I still struggle to spell like *balloon, significant, dessert* vs *desert* (I still don't know which one is which), and *separate* will always be correct and none shall be the wiser... except for those of you reading this book. Please don't tell anyone.

Rule #62
Nervous passengers should just close their eyes.

I'm a little bit of a control freak. Not excessive, but just enough to drive my wife crazy. When I'm the passenger I like to know when the car is going to turn and at what speed. I like to know exactly which lane the vehicle is going to be in, and I don't trust anyone else to do it correctly.

You may have already figured out which person you are in this scenario. Maybe some of you can keep calm and drive on, but it's usually one spouse or the other that is as crazy as me. It drives my wife batty when I throw my hands up on the dashboard (bracing myself for a horrific collision) while she's driving. My dad was the same way before me. He tried to play it cool though. He would get scared, make a quick movement, and then pretend he was tying his shoe, or slap the door and pretend he was making sure it was locked. It never fooled anyone, but it was cute. Me, I'm not so cute. I just dramatically slap the windows, doors, and roof, and it's usually accompanied by a grunt or a scream that sounds like a four-year-old girl.

At any rate, it causes about eighty percent of the arguments between us and is one of those relationship issues that may never be fully resolved. You just have to find a way to cope with it. Sorry honey, when you're behind the wheel, I should just take a deep breath, lean my seat back, and close my eyes.

Rule #63

People come in all kinds of wrappers.

Thankfully my wife loves me just as I am. I keep saying this but she knew what she was getting when she said yes. It's my attempt to make her feel better about her choice of a husband!

I am terrible at gift-wrapping. If I concentrate, I can do fair. The problem is the last sentence. I absolutely do not concentrate on, nor care about, gift-wrapping. I don't pick out the right paper, I cram in the tissue stuff and it just looks like an accident. It looks like a cat tried to make a bed, moved a bunch of stuff around, and then threw in a gift as an afterthought.

My kids gift wrap much better than I do. Especially the girl kids. They take their time, they line up the edges, and they use a small amount of tape. I am the opposite on all of those things.

Also, this goes along with it, but I am a terrible card chooser. We buy one of those large industrial cases of cards that have every imaginable occasion inside, and I never choose the right one according to my wife. She's right. I choose the wrong color, the wrong occasion, the wrong size envelope. I'm just deficient in this department.

Despite all of these important shortcomings, my wife still loves me and we have both learned that either she or the girl offspring are the best ones to make any decisions regarding gifts.

I suppose the real remedy is to care more and to take more time, but I have the attention span of a... what was I saying?

Rule #64

Figure out who is in the driver's seat... literally.

My wife would make a great Boy Scout. Or Navy Seal. Or Secret Agent. She could be dropped in the middle of the woods and would use the tools of nature to survive. I, on the other hand, really enjoy camping... at a Hilton. We are very different in that way and we knew all of this going into marriage.

When it comes to driving and directions there are age-old roles that we fall into. Guys don't like to ask for directions and women don't like to get lost. Okay, perhaps these are gross generalizations. However it breaks down in your marriage, you need to decide who is doing which roles early on. It will be maddening for everyone involved if both assume they are the pilot—or worse, both think they are the navigator. This is bad news for not only the driver but also all of the passengers, including the kids who end up screaming and fighting in the back seat while you try to figure out where in the world you're going.

Shortly into marriage, my wife and I went on a trip to Europe. Way back in the early 2000s we did not have the option to navigate by smartphone nor rely on a portable GPS. Instead she navigated our entire trip using the sun, sheer instinct, and some really lousy maps from the AAA. I was impressed. I know the general rules. The sun rises in the east and sets in the west but that's about it. She could accurately tell the time of day and all kinds of other insane things just by looking up.

We drove through twelve countries in three weeks. It was a crazy, fun-filled journey that I wouldn't trade for anything. She is amazing at navigation and I am horrible. Admitting I have a problem is step one, right? And the fact that I can say that out loud means that we probably have a healthy marriage in this department.

Now, it's time for another one of those "Ryan did it wrong" stories. The setting was Palm Springs, California. I was in the driver's seat and trying to navigate from our restaurant back to the hotel. I was getting information from both my wife and my dad who was sitting in the backseat. In the midst of all of the commotion, I somehow disregarded some moderately important signage about a one-way street. I suddenly had screaming from inside the car, horn honking and yelling from outside the car, and it was pure chaos. I threw the car in park and jumped out refusing to drive another mile with this sort of insurrection happening in my vehicle.

In retrospect, maybe, just maybe I should not have gone down a one-way street the wrong way, and it sounds a little bit like it was all my fault. At any rate, now you know my wife is a great navigator and I've been known to jump out of a car under pressure. Know your roles.

Rule #65

R-E-S-P-E-C-T –find out what it means.

The other night as the kids were going to bed, my wife gave them some very specific directions. I strolled in a few minutes later and offered completely different instructions. It all had to do with whether or not they could stay up and read books before it was time for lights out. I thought it was a good plan and would help them fall asleep quicker, but my wife knew this would only prolong their bedtime routine. She had music ready to go and they had all agreed to her terms until I came along.

Understandably, she was frustrated because I had just undermined her discipline. Then I made the mistake of saying, "I have been a parent for the same amount of time that you have!" FYI: that's not a good thing to say. Take it from me. Thankfully, the first thing we did was agree on a game plan in front of the kids and presented a united front until we could take the conversation behind closed doors.

As we discussed this parenting and marital faux pas, I realized that she has a much different perspective on parenting because she is home with them all day. She has to deal with the reality of what will happen if they don't get enough sleep.

I learned that I need to respect her expertise on the little things that turn into really big things, and she learned that I have an opinion on the matter, even though it may be wrong. Respecting each other in private and in public is essential. And now Aretha Franklin's song is stuck in my head.

Happily Ever After

Rule #66

Eat, pray, love, and avoid the flan.

Traveling with your spouse is something I can't recommend enough. Experiencing new places and new adventures will strengthen your bond while creating memories to last a lifetime. Whether it be a family vacation with kids in tow or a trip with just the two of you, your marriage will definitely benefit.

Our walls at home are covered with photos from fun trips. One of my favorite memories is being on the beach in the Grand Cayman Islands with my wife at a little spot called Rum Point. There were hammocks in the trees and turquoise water as far as the eye could see. We both decided that day that we had to quit our jobs and move there immediately. We even went as far as driving around scouting out land for sale to build our little beach shack on. Then reality set in, and we returned to our lives with photos and memories in tow.

Unfortunately not all travel stories are good ones. A friend of mine told me about a childhood trip she went on with her family. Her dad had always wanted to take the whole family on a cross-country train ride. Unfortunately there was a food poisoning issue in the dining car a couple days into the trip and the dream vacation sort of turned into a regurgitating nightmare.

Another story that is forever stuck in my mind is from some married friends of ours who were vacationing in Mexico a few years back. While strolling down a charming street after dinner one night, the tropical breeze carried the sweet aroma of something irresistible. It was flan, the sugary custard dessert popular in Mexico. But this was no ordinary custard, this was street flan, from a street vendor. With street repercussions. We don't need to go into detail about what the next three days consisted of, but while he was passed out on the bathroom floor, his wife spent as much time out and about by herself because the hotel room was small and filled with a permeating smell. Hey, they had paid for a vacation so someone might as well have enjoyed it.

For the most part vacations are relaxing, and making lasting memories with your spouse will benefit your marriage. Just don't forget your passport, use bottled water, and avoid the street flan at all costs.

Rule #67

Stop keeping virtual score.

It starts with an innocent comment comparing your day's events to that of your spouse's. The next thing you know, you are caught up in a vicious one-up battle between husband and wife. And nothing is as awkward as sitting at the dinner table between another couple while they battle it out placing points on their virtual scoreboard.

> Him: "Oh, you think your day was hard; try driving home in bumper-to-bumper traffic!"
>
> Her: "That sounds like a vacation to me! Try staying at home with three fussy kids. Stuck in a car alone sounds fantastic!"
>
> Him: "Oh yeah, try getting chewed out by your boss, then having six back-to-back meetings! I would love to spend money all day and stroll around the store."
>
> Her: "More like race to the store to buy paper towels so I can wipe spit up off the floor where the baby barfed all morning."

Meanwhile you are choking down your dinner trying not to make eye contact or take sides as the couple verbally dukes it out.

I would call it one-upping each other, but it's really more like one-downing because you're fighting over who has it worse. I don't actually remember when it first began, probably when the kids came along, but my wife and I got sucked into the game of who got less sleep. Then it became who had less to eat or didn't get to eat at all, who had a harder day, and my personal favorite, who is more sick.

This game is difficult to resist and highly addictive, but it's a slippery slope once you begin keeping score. Remember you are in this together and if you don't play like a team, it's game over.

Rule #68
If you have a smart phone, don't be a dumb spouse.

Technology, when used the right way, makes our lives run smoothly, keeps us in communication with the ones we love, and, in my opinion, just makes a lot of things more fun. Take grocery shopping for instance. When my wife and I were first married, we would go to the grocery store together. She would grab a cart, and I would make a beeline for the magazine aisle. I loathed shopping, and this mildly irritated my wife. Then along came the smartphone with smart little apps like a grocery shopping list that lets me scan barcodes and check things off as I go. I'm awesome at shopping now, and my wife couldn't be happier with my enthusiasm.

On the flipside, if you allow them to, phones and computer devices can drive a wedge between couples. Social media, games, and web surfing has become a modern addiction and I am the first to admit that it is hard to resist. When I'm traveling, I use mobile technology constantly because it is an easy way to stay connected. When I return home, it can be difficult to wean myself off these devices. The problem is every time I pick up or look at the little gadget, I am taking my attention away from my family. I make it a point to leave my phone in another room during mealtimes and when I'm playing with my kids to make sure they know my attention is focused on them.

Several friends have complained (wives to be specific) about their spouse picking up a mobile phone and surfing the web in the middle of a conversation. You might as well turn your back and walk out of the room because it basically sends the same message to the person who is trying to connect with you. And absolutely under no circumstances should you start surfing the web while reading this book. I will know if you do.

Even worse, being secretive with your devices, having inappropriate content and apps, deleting texts and history, etc. leads you down a slippery slope of mistrust and jealousy that can ultimately destroy your marriage. Ironically enough, there are apps you can download that hold you accountable for this kind of destructive behavior. The bottom line is to use your judgement and exercise self-control.

One of my favorite advances in electronic devices is the GPS function. I not only use it when I'm on the road for navigation purposes, but it has given my wife and me the ability to keep up with each other through the use of various friend-finding apps. I imagine in the early days a caveman would have to send up some sort of smoke signal when he got where he was going, or face being clubbed by an angry worried cavewoman when he returned. Now that there are apps for tracking locations, my wife can see that I made it to my destination and ease her concerns any time she needs to. I can't imagine any situation my wife and I would have, short of a surprise party, where we would ever feel the need to conceal our location from one another.

No secrets. End of story.

Rule #69
You will realize this is not the person you married.

It would be ridiculous to expect my seven-year-old to still eat baby food or my five-year-old to drink breast milk from a bottle; yet, many of us are surprised when we realize a decade or so into marriage that this is not the person we fell in love with and married.

Here's the spoiler: people change. There you have it, the ultimate truth about a successful marriage. The sooner we realize that change is inevitable, the better off we will be knowing that it is okay, and we can continue to love each other through it.

Circumstances happen. Life happens. I changed, my wife changed, my kids have definitely changed, and the quicker we get over the selfish longing for that neophyte you started marriage with, the better off we'll be.

Just as a test, go back and look at your wedding photos. Look at your hair. Look at that tuxedo and the baby face on both of you! Styles have definitely changed. Some of the people in that wedding party you don't even talk to anymore, and we have all gotten wiser.

After all, do you really want to do life with that novice spouse you married long ago? You have been through a war together, people. You have fought bravely. You've been through thick and thin, sickness and health, and you are stronger, better people for it! Love your spouse for the person they have become.

Rule #70   Choose a Cause.

Living in the first world we can easily get into a routine of doing things a particular way at a particular time and not breaking out. Left unchecked, it can eventually lead us to a self-centered lifestyle that is unhealthy. As an antidote, you should find a charity or a cause that the whole family can be a part of and tackle it together.

There are lots of great options. I read one story recently of a local family that decided to make burritos to feed the homeless. Mom, dad, and kids worked to make the ingredients and assemble the burritos and together served over 55,000 meals to the inner city homeless.

There are amazing child sponsorship programs, rescue organizations, and hands-on charities that your family can be a part of. In suburban Los Angeles, there is a charity that uses local volunteers to help package food to send overseas to kids in desperate need of nutrition. Your family can work together for just a few hours to make a positive impact, all the while having some cell phone-free quality time to laugh, talk, and work alongside each other. This sort of undivided attention within the family is practically unheard of these days. It will bring your family closer together, guaranteed.

Rule #71

Make 'em laugh.

On the back cover of this book I promised you that I have the secret to a happy marriage. I, Ryan O'Quinn, hold the key to happily ever after. Ready for it? Here it is... laugh! There you have it. Now before you go begging for your money back, just hear me out.

I remember the day I discovered I could be funny. I was at the dinner table and I said something that made my parents lose their breaths laughing. Best of all, I remember I wasn't even trying to make them laugh; I just happened to tell a funny story.

For the most part, all of us experience the same general things in life. How we handle those things is what makes the difference and determines the amount of joy we get to experience. We can choose to be glass-half-empty people, or we can roll with it and laugh out loud.

Studies have shown that laughing actually gives you a longer life. We know it is a panacea for illness. I'm here to tell you it can not only prolong your life, it can actually save your marriage. Just laugh. After all, what is the alternative?

Quick reference guide

Do something! Marriage requires effort, so here are a few ideas of what you can do together to make your marriage better than ever.

Read this book out loud!

Take a massage class

Picnic in the park

Take a walk as often as possible

Try something new

Take a dance class

Hold hands every chance you get

Find a sport to play

Start an air guitar band

Steal a kiss

Go dancing

Ride bikes

Take a cooking class

Volunteer

Fly a kite

Play mini golf

See a movie in the park

Play pool

Go to a "pick your own" fruit farm

Start a game night

Compliment each other regularly

Go to the driving range

Race go-carts

Watch the sunset

See a double feature

Go to an amusement park

Plan a trip

Be spontaneous

Go on a hike

Go swimming

Throw a ball back and forth

Play charades